ESCAPE

from

RWANDA

ESCAPE
from
RWANDA

A true story of faith, hope, and survival

John Yves Bizimana

DESERET
BOOK

SALT LAKE CITY, UTAH

Library of Congress Cataloging-in-Publication Data

Bizimana, John.
    Escape from Rwanda : a true story of faith, hope, and survival / John Bizimana.
        p. cm.
    Includes bibliographical references.
    ISBN 978-1-60641-830-7 (hardbound : alk. paper)
    1. Bizimana, John. 2. Refugees—Rwanda—Biography. 3. Rwanda—History—Civil War, 1994—Personal narratives. 4. Refugees—Belgium—Biography. 5. Mormon converts—Belgium—Biography. I. Title.
    DT450.437.B59 A3 2010
    967.57104'31—dc22
    [B]   2010022027

Printed in the United States of America
Publishers Printing, Salt Lake City, UT

10   9   8   7   6   5   4   3   2   1

*To anyone who ever had a dream but knew no means
to make it come true; to the honor of Angel and Mary Yvette,
who have endured all and conquered all with me; and to the
memory of Thérèse Mukakabera, my angel mother*

◆◇◆

CONTENTS

◇◈◇

ACKNOWLEDGMENTS

I would like to thank the following individuals: Kaylynn Wakefield, for giving me the idea; Courtney Lyn Jensen Peacock, one of the very first to see the manuscript and for her resulting invaluable insight; Colleen Whitley, whose tireless and faithful efforts gave the manuscript the ultimate edge; Jana Erickson, for giving me a shot at telling my story; Derk Koldewyn, for his keen eye and skill in helping me tell this story in the best possible way; and Spencer and Kelly Kimball, who took a chance on me and made this story possible. Finally, I would like to thank Chris Chileshe Jr., Regina Mukondola, Patrick Muir, Gail Halladay, Leigh Dethman, and Roberta Stout.

INTRODUCTION

I am a college student and in many ways the typical college student. I would rather prolong my sleeping hours on a Monday morning than attend an early-morning class. As part of my college ritual, I worry about deadlines, midterms, and finals, and I dread essays like the plague. Some semesters have been successful, and others less so. In fact, my failure in one semester was so spectacular I was convinced my professors were forming a secret alliance to plot my expulsion from school. Like most other college students, I wrestled over what my field of study would be, and I finally chose economics. My reasoning was simple. First, I find economics fascinating, and second, perhaps more important, economics may be the shortest major at Brigham Young University. I am overwhelmed by the impression that most of what I have learnt in college, especially the mandatory general courses, I will not use in real life. I am convinced that five minutes after graduation, the only concept I will remember will be supply and demand, and that will be the end of it.

My fellow classmates are mostly from Utah, Idaho, California, Nevada, Washington, Texas, Virginia, or just somewhere on the East Coast of the United States. Many of them have never ventured beyond the United States, and when they hear the stories I tell about the countries I have visited and the number of languages I speak, they suppose me the son of a diplomat or a military man, and I am besieged with countless questions. On those occasions, I cease being a typical American college student as I am asked to tell my story.

My story, like any other, is one of life's adventures seen through my eyes. It is a story of change, the kind that calls upon you when your life seems ill-suited for upheaval. As much as I have suffered, so have I learnt, among other things, that in the face of difficulties I never found strength until I withdrew from looking outward and began looking inward for inspiration. Those times, those seasons that sealed my youth with a curse, were both glorious and treacherous. Though at first my struggles seemed a curse that often caused me to bury my face in the shallow grave of the palms of my hands, they have since blessed the path of my life. Once it was said of me, "There goes the boy who dwindled in the swamps of desolation—alas, he walks in reckoning of life's debt to him." I now walk to demand the best there is in life. I have examined my past and pondered the trials that confounded me like an ant stranded in the mighty Amazon. What ennobling sentiments can I relate about a victory well won? What are the best lessons that I have learnt from a life driven by change?

Introduction

This has been my quest: to find meaning in the dual challenges that have long consumed my life—wealth and poverty, peace and war, victory and defeat, joy and grief, and most important, life and death. In the natural consequence of an incredible past, I have often petitioned the Lord to equip me with the means to inspire my peers and to arm them with the knowledge that they can rise above the present, regardless of the past, if only they can make hope their fire. To that end, I have composed an account of my life to this point. While in some respects its only requirement amounted to a mere walk down memory lane, therein lies the challenge of accuracy, which I am certain I have not completely overcome. Nevertheless, the hardest thing I ever have had to do was to believe that I could accomplish what I have now accomplished. That dreams do come true is my testimony, as is the story of my life, a life that was preserved by the hand of divine providence, that I might one day share this story.

Chapter 1

BEGINNINGS

I was born in Kigali, the capital city of Rwanda, on the first day of August 1986. When I was six years old, my father, disregarding my tender age, shoved me into my first challenge. It all began when an acquaintance of my father's—probably a business associate—paid a visit to our home. Our visitor had traveled to see us by bicycle, an old-fashioned but common black model which was very popular with the villagers. I had been watching a children's show on television when one of our domestic workers announced our visitor. My father, who had been reading a newspaper, stepped outside, and I joined him to welcome our visitor. I watched with fascination as this tall African man dismounted his bicycle and carefully leaned it against the wall. The man approached my father, all smiles, with both his arms outstretched to initiate the traditional Rwandan greeting of grasping the other's arms at the elbow while gently touching foreheads three times.

While they exchanged pleasantries, my eyes remained glued

to that remarkable vehicle. I longed for a chance to have a go at it. I did not own one, not for lack of means but perhaps only because there was no ground fit for a bicycle in our yard. My father turned to me to bid me greet our visitor. He noticed me staring and then shifted his gaze to the bicycle. He glanced back at me, sensing the urge raging in me. He squatted down to my height and asked me if I wanted to learn to ride a bicycle.

"Yes," I replied. "I want to ride that one," and I pointed to our visitor's bicycle. My father talked briefly with the man, who offered profusely to put it at my disposal. Without hesitation, my father swept me from the ground, my feet arching to cling to my flip-flops. He lifted me onto the bicycle while our visitor held it steady. The seat was far too tall for my legs; I could not sit on it and reach the pedals at the same time. I resembled a circus attraction with my precarious footing and inappropriate footwear. My father confidently guided me out onto the main brown dirt road, prepping me by arousing my sense of pride. He said that only a man could bear the dangers that I was about to assume. My hands clutched the handlebars tightly; my face was locked in concentration. My father suddenly broke into a trot, then a full sprint, and pushed me forward down the road as he released his grip on the bike. He managed to yell out, "Be careful!" as I dashed uncertainly down the road with cars approaching from the opposite direction.

I was utterly terrified. I pedaled frantically to keep up as the bicycle zigzagged, following my unsteady hands. Luckily, the momentum my father had transferred to me was enough to keep me propelled a distance on my side of the road. I did not quite understand the braking system. An idea flashed before me: To stop, I would need to collide into something. I was lucky to spot a fence ahead that I ran into and toppled over, falling off the bicycle onto a soft patch of grass. My flip-flops were still on my feet, though the wind had been knocked out of me. The bicycle lay nearby.

An amused bystander helped me lift the bicycle up, and we pushed it back toward home until we met my applauding father, who had followed me halfway. "Now, do you want to do it again?" he teased. I just shook my head. I was still catching my breath, panting. I felt like a champion despite my failure to master the art of riding a bicycle.

My father's extreme methods were not uncommon. I would not have been surprised if he had thrown me in the ocean in order to teach me to swim. The lesson, however, was clear: sometimes you do not need to thrive in or master a particularly challenging situation. Merely surviving it is enough.

◨

My immediate family was composed of my father, Jean-Baptiste, my mother, Thérèse, my younger sister, Mary Yvette, and my younger brother Ange, whom we call Angel today. Mary is two years younger than I, and Angel is a year younger than she.

My father was an ambitious man, and by the standards of his time and place he enjoyed a great deal of prosperity. He worked for a company that marketed Toyota vehicles and was known to bring home a different car every so often. I cannot recall exactly how tall he was, but his lean physique is still fresh in my memory. From those who knew him, I understand he was somewhat short. He was quite dark in complexion, and his captivating smile revealed perfectly straight white teeth. It has always been a puzzle to me that I was not genetically predisposed to inherit this feature; neither did I inherit his height (or lack of it). My mother was an accountant for the major hospital in Kigali. She was a small woman and quite distinctly so. Those who referred to her would designate her as the "small lady from so-and-so." She was fairer in complexion than my father and had a stout, athletic body. If one were to refer to her features, her smile would eclipse everything else, for her smile was one to forever remember.

We led a life of relative ease. We had a huge house with many rooms. It had acres of woods, well-kept green lawns, a thriving vegetable garden, and a cottage. A trail of vividly colored flowers led to the portal of our red brick house. This trail was set in smooth stones that crunched when trod upon. A huge gray stone wall with broken glass cemented into the top to keep out burglars enclosed our home. The only point of entry was a solid red metal gate that creaked loudly when opened. A security guard attended it. We had an army of domestic workers to maintain the house and tend to all of our needs. Because of the prestige and appearance of our home, rumors spread like wildfire that it was the residence of a rich white man. The power that humanity ascribes to appearances is indeed ridiculously significant. In the early 1990s, before the Rwandan genocide, that appearance was the difference between an intact home and a looted one when riots and civil war broke out. No one would have dared to loot a rich white man's house. Despite a few episodes of civil unrest, I have learnt from my extended family that Rwanda was then a relatively peaceful country.

My father and I were the best of friends. Almost every weekend, he took my brother Angel and me to soccer games at the nearby stadium. On these days my sister, Mary, would stay home with my mother. My father carried a playful attitude that he extended to most aspects of his life. He enjoyed interacting with our domestic workers while watching highly anticipated soccer games on television. Our living room would be rowdy with cheers, jeers, and raucous laughter while they all drank down kegs of beer. They would argue about who was the best soccer player in the world. My father's favorite athlete was the Argentinian great, Diego Maradona. He even bought me a pair of Maradona sneakers, which I dutifully wore to every soccer game that we attended.

After a rowdy soccer game on television, the domestic workers would leave, and my mother would spoil us with a simple but delicious meal. It usually included plantains, a fruit from the

John's father, Jean-Baptiste, with John's siblings, Angel, age three, and Mary Yvette, age four, in Rwanda, 1992. This is the first picture John was allowed to take with his father's camera.

banana family. This was my father's favorite. He would rub his hands together with glee and vocalize a prolonged "hoouuuuu" at receiving this meal of sorts. On occasion, when my mother wasn't looking, he would sneak up behind her and poke her in the ribs. She would jolt upright and shoot him a stern look. Then she would just shake her head, and he would in turn shrug his shoulders with impunity.

He also enjoyed taking pictures of his children, especially when we were in odd positions, our silly deeds immortalized to be recalled at will. His camera was like his fourth child; he never allowed anyone to touch it. I felt very fortunate once when he allowed me to take a picture of him, Mary, and Angel. I deemed it a great honor to be entrusted with such a responsibility. He was our ally, ever having fun.

My mother was the strict disciplinarian. One Sunday she prepared us to attend church. When it was time to leave, my father was watching the Arnold Schwarzenegger movie *Commando* with a number of his friends in our living room. I told my mother that I wanted to stay behind and watch the movie as well. She immediately started castigating my father, saying, "Now look: Yves wants to behave like you. Go get ready for church and be a good example!" My father just chuckled, told me to go to church with Mother, and remained with his friends, much to her disappointment. Later, we found him in the congregation, well-groomed to fit the occasion. My mother's words had worked on him. I was surprised by my mother's audacity. She sometimes talked to him in the same way she talked to us.

In spite of his nonchalance, my father was an austere teacher. Life-governing principles were the one area in which his carefree

John's parents' wedding, Rwanda, 1986. From left to right:
John's paternal grandparents; his father, Jean-Baptiste; his mother,
Thérèse; his maternal grandparents.

attitude ended and his wisdom began. He taught me about generosity one day when I had a brawl with my brother, Angel. Whenever my father bought a new piece of electronic equipment, I would collect the white polystyrene packing material and mold it into pistols and other kinds of toys. Angel would then try to claim them as his own. He would justify this by pointing out that I had more than I could use. At such times, we would erupt in bitter contention— until the day that my father intervened. He made me understand that nothing is really yours that you cannot give away; that which you cannot give away makes you equal to its worth. Such was my father's philosophy, and this is the prevailing attitude in many African societies. Nowhere else in the world will you find generosity such as you will find in the poor communities of poor countries.

My family was large. I had uncles and aunts, grandfathers and grandmothers, godparents, first cousins, and second cousins. We always had a house full of family members coming and going. My father's younger sister, Aunt Jeanine, lived permanently with us. It is the custom in Rwanda, and in other African countries generally, that when you fare well for yourself, you have an obligation to help less-privileged relatives. I have learnt that nothing gave more pride to my father than building his parents a home at the first stroke of his success. I suppose that my father's success stemmed from his education and inclination to hard work. In his family, he was among the first generation of literate men. The same was true of my mother in her family. No one in the generations before them ever knew when he or she had been born, coming no closer to their own birthdays than "around the time when this or that great event happened."

We could say that we had the world at our feet. Life was bliss. All was well. In the innocence of youth, I thought that life would always continue in that manner. I knew of no other way to live than in the security of my loving parents, large family, and considerable ease. The hardest ordeals I underwent had been waiting impatiently for a late chauffeur at school or unintentionally drowning my pet birds when I tried to teach them to swim. Little did I know that this idyllic life was an illusion that would not sustain itself for long.

On December 30, 1993, my father was on his way home from work for the lunch break. As he drove through Kigali, his car collided head-on with a truck. By the time medics reached him, he was already dead. He left this world at thirty-three years of age, but in my seven-year-old eyes, it would not be fully clear to me what had happened until he was buried. My mother, my Aunt Jeanine, my siblings Mary and Angel, and I were at home that day. I do not recall how I was occupying my time in my room, but I distinctly remember hearing an unusual wailing coming from the living room. Someone had come to deliver the tragic news. Curious, I left my room and found Aunt Jeanine pacing the room wailing and exclaiming dramatically, "It's finished! It's finished!" I did not understand what was happening.

My mother digested stoically the bitter unveiling of our new reality. I suppose she wanted to remain strong for us, but she later burst into emotion at the descent of my father's casket into the earth.

The cleaned body was brought into our home some hours after the accident, and my father was laid in his former bedroom. I sneaked in to be with him. His body was resting in an open casket. I peered at his face and noticed some bruises on his forehead, but they had been tended to. I looked down and noticed his feet sticking out of the casket. I was convinced that I had a foolproof plan to

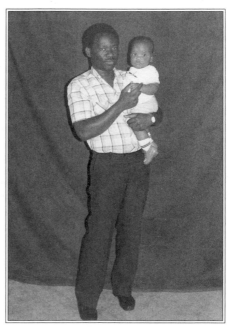

John, age about one, and his father, Jean-Baptiste, in Rwanda, 1987.

wake him up. We had similar big toes, and I thought that if I pulled his hard enough, he would spring from his slumber, mimicking the countless times in the past I had unfailingly awakened him in that manner.

To my disappointment, the spell did not break, and he slept on in eternity. I sat there, feeling terribly sorry for myself, thinking, "Now there is no one to take me to soccer games anymore." In time I would realize that I had lost the largest part of me, the being through whom, until then, I had defined myself.

◘

My father was buried in his home village on the next day, New Year's Eve, 1994. Owing to his absence thereafter and never having had the chance to form an intimate knowledge of his character, I have since undertaken to re-create it myself. I like to believe that my father was an honorable man of the noblest character. I like to believe that he espoused principles of equality and fairness and that had the war caught up to him, his actions would have inspired the utmost admiration and respect. I like to believe that he honored his word and that he treated my mother as tenderly as is humanly possible. Finally, I like to believe that he esteemed nothing more worthy or more dear to him than the integrity of his family. Unfortunately or fortunately, I have been relieved of the possibility of finding out if my belief was the truth. I barely knew him, yet I loved him. Though at that time I concluded that his death was absolutely the worst tragedy that could befall a young boy like me, I was to learn that it was only the beginning of a turbulent childhood that no child should ever have to endure.

Chapter 2

RWANDA

The dawn of the year 1994 found my family's spirits depressed. I do not recall any celebrations, laughter, or joy, but I do recall deep feelings of sadness. Even more distressing was the prospect of what the loss of my father meant for my family. As for my personal inclination, I was deeply uncertain of everything. I did not know what was real and what was not. As far back as I could remember, nothing had been more certain than my father; in nothing had I exercised more faith than I had in my father. Seeing his casket being buried in the earth had dispelled whatever hope I harbored of ever seeing him again. Death imposed a nonnegotiable finality, and as far as I was concerned, my father would never live again.

Days, weeks, a month, and then another month came and went. My mother slowly found her way as family and friends offered support, shouldering some of her burdens. Her coping seemed sound, at least as sound as the judgment of a seven-year-old can fathom. In due time, the financial stability that had followed my father's name vanished, and inevitable changes overtook my family. We moved into a smaller house, and life became quieter with the departure of our domestic workers. I also lost half my toys in the move, a blow that unsettled me greatly.

As much as we may want to lengthen or shorten our time in any one moment or phase of our lives, whether joyful or sad, at length life does go on. Around this time my mother started taking driving classes. She had not learnt to drive because when my father was not driving her around, a chauffeur had taken his place. Now she wanted to be independent, so she spent long hours practicing with an instructor. Sometimes she allowed me to go and watch her; I was the designated judge of her progress. Looking back, I am impressed with the strength of her character. She did not put her life on hold to fully mourn her husband but carried on with her responsibilities. I suppose that my father's absence allowed her to grow and find her own courage and independence, qualities that she would need for what lay ahead.

I noticed a trend in my mother's behavior: she started spending more time with us, her children. In the evenings we would huddle together to listen to the news and to a few Michael Jackson records. He had been my father's absolute idol, and on quite a few occasions my father requested that I perform Michael Jackson's famous "moonwalk" for him and his friends. After my execution of this move, they would all applaud, and my father would boast about me all day. In those evenings of serene reminiscence, we would feel like my father was very much alive.

On one such evening, April 6, 1994, we heard the sound of

an explosion in the distance. We asked our mother what it was. She was unsure. Then we heard the sound of distant gunfire, and we rushed out to see orange streaks of light darting across the starry sky. "What are those?" I asked pointing to the sky.

"Bullets," my mother replied. She hurriedly ushered us back into the house. She told us to gather all the mattresses from our beds and prop them along the walls of the corridors. I later understood that it was to prevent stray bullets from easily piercing the walls and windows. We huddled together in our corridor. Occasionally we heard clanking sounds outside our house and wondered if we were in proximity to those bullets. No one slept a wink that night. I lay there on my back staring into the dark, listening tensely for the next shots.

By daybreak the sound of shooting had died down. We stepped out into the yard to find a number of used bullets scattered around. We also spotted some places on our walls where bullets had ended their trajectory.

We later heard on the radio that the airplane carrying the president of Rwanda had been shot down. What ensued was complete mayhem. At the time, I was still too young to understand the political situation of the country.

Even today, the identity of those responsible for shooting down the president's plane remains unclear. What is clear is the reality of the oldest story in human history. Two or more people in coexistence will always clash at some point or another. Though opinions differ, all Rwandan people that I have questioned agree that there were perennial tensions between the two native ethnic groups of Hutus and Tutsis before the genocide.

That night was the culmination of a history of power struggles between the two ethnic groups.

I have heard the notion that Rwandans were once a reasonably united people. I don't know that they were actually united. I think it was more a case of respecting each other's turf; they may not have been completely peaceful, but at least they could get along with each other. That uneasy peace existed until the Belgian colonizers came and played on what they observed to be differences between these two groups. The Belgians emphasized those differences in their strategy of dividing in order to conquer. Conquerors, politicians, and manipulators of all kinds seldom get away with actually inventing anything new; their strength lies in recognizing what existing situations they can exploit.

In the early 1920s, the Belgians were granted a mandate to govern what was then known as Ruanda-Urundi by the League of Nations. Rwanda as we know it now—or as I knew it as a child—did not, as yet, exist. The Belgians then installed the Tutsi minority as the ruling class over the large Hutu majority. In the mid-1920s, the Belgians introduced a system of identity cards that classified different segments of the Rwandan population into ethnic groups, thus magnifying ethnic consciousness. From then on, ethnic strife became a common occurrence.

In the late 1950s, the Hutus rebelled against the Belgian colonizers and the Tutsi elite, causing the displacement, or diaspora, of a large Tutsi population. Among the crucial events that took place at this time was that groups both inside and outside Rwanda—including Rwandan citizens, diplomats with the United Nations, and others involved in the Pan-African movement—were demanding free elections, which the Belgians finally were required to allow. The first election was held in 1960, the year my father was born, and that election, not surprisingly, moved the Hutus into power. They were the overwhelming majority.

It is also important to note that the Belgians—pushed by the U.N.—granted full independence in the 1960s to the African nations they had colonized. For Rwanda, the date of independence was July 1, 1962. My good friend Colleen Whitley, whom I call Grandma Colleen, remembers watching the news on American television as the Belgian flag came down and the flags of such African nations as the Congo went up. It was all lovely, with bands playing and people smiling. One of the U.S. news commentators noted that the groundwork for independence had not been laid, and doubtless a bloodbath would follow. This prediction proved accurate. A few weeks later that same news show carried footage of massacres.

By the early to mid-1960s, the Hutus retained all power in Rwanda, and the Tutsi diaspora became as large and significant as the Tutsi presence in Rwanda. Military campaigns in Rwanda spearheaded by Tutsis in exile heightened tensions between the two ethnicities, culminating in periodic massacres in the 1960s and 1970s.

By the early 1990s, the Hutu president was compelled by international pressure to negotiate with the Tutsis in a deal to allow the Tutsis in exile to return to Rwanda and to form a coalition government with them. By late 1993 and early 1994, however, a general sense of anxiety pervaded the country as hate media and political rhetoric incited violence. Then the Hutu president's plane was shot down, an event generally recognized as the catalyst of the Rwandan genocide.

In the hearts of many, the events that led to that fateful night are a matter of great sensitivity, and I would not wish to be inaccurate. What I have described is a brief sketch of the situation as portrayed by the literature I have consulted. More complete histories can be found in books of the caliber of *Origins of Rwandan Genocide* by Josias Semujanga (Amherst, N.Y.: Humanity Books, 2003), or *An Ordinary Man,* the autobiography of Paul Rusesabagina (New York: Viking, 2006), the source of the well-known Hollywood movie *Hotel Rwanda.*

I would have liked to know my mother's opinion on the matter because I did not have one for myself. I was just a bewildered kid trying to make sense of it all. I cannot remember how long we lived in uncertainty and fear before we heard loud banging on our gates followed by shouts demanding that we open them. My mother and aunt panicked, not knowing if it was an enemy at the gates or friends.

As the banging persisted, they resolved that they had no choice but to open the gates. It was no secret to them that the gates could be forced open easily. My mother went to open them and instructed us to stay inside with Aunt Jeanine, who kept us calm. We stood watching by the window as my mother hesitantly proceeded towards the gates. With a little effort she unfastened the latch, and the gates were pushed wide open.

Half a dozen soldiers in green uniforms and with rifles slung over their shoulders entered our front yard. I noticed a small commotion beyond the opened gates. I was not sure what it was. The commanding officer started talking to my mother with his rifle slung over his shoulder and pointed at her while the rest of his troops checked the yard. I instinctively broke free of my aunt's grip and bolted outside to my mother. As I burst through the door, she turned and drew me close to her. I stood protectively in front of her with my back against her legs and her arms around my neck. I stared defiantly into the muzzle that was pointed at her while the officer observed half-amused.

He barked orders to the rest of his troops, and they went into our house and started searching it. My aunt stood inside with her arms around Mary and Angel. When the soldiers were satisfied with their inspection of our home, the commanding officer instructed us to pack what we could and evacuate. He told us we should go to the nearby stadium for our own protection. The situation had become dangerous, he said, and everyone was going to that stadium. Under the scrutiny of the soldiers, my mother quickly packed some clothes. We took all of our electronics that were worth anything and piled them into the trunk of our car.

We all got into the car with my mother at the wheel. Good thing she had been taking driving lessons. The soldiers watched us as we drove out into the driveway. We left them loitering around our yard and in our house. We were surprised to see that we were not alone in this evacuation. Hundreds and hundreds of people were heading to the same destination, which was usually only about fifteen minutes away. Our car crawled into the line of men, women, children, cows, goats, chickens, cars, wagons, and possibly wheelbarrows. We stared in disbelief at women and men carrying their belongings in huge bags. Some women were carrying their toddlers. We could tell that most of these people

Arrival of Rwandan refugees in Ngara District, Kagera Region, Tanzania, April 1994. Photo courtesy UNHCR.

had been rushed out of their homes, judging by the half-naked children we saw and other evidence of the chaotic nature of the evacuation. We inched our way to the stadium through the throngs and finally reached the parking lot. My mother found a parking spot, and we stepped out and took our bags.

We then scrambled to acquire a space we could call our own. We hustled around, dragging our bags among the crowds. We were lucky to find refuge with a family that my mother knew. They had already secured a room for themselves. The stadium had some rooms in it that I suppose were usually reserved for distinguished individuals during soccer games, but they suited our purpose at the time.

We lived there for a number of days; I cannot remember how many. I was only seven years of age. I spent those days running around with Angel, who was four, and Mary, who was five, and some other little friends that I had made. My mother never permitted us to venture far. I even befriended some soldiers from Bangladesh who were stationed in Rwanda as U.N. peacekeepers. They taught me the basics of their language, and I was fascinated by how you could say the same thing in different languages. This must have instilled in me the passion I have for languages. I am fascinated by all kinds of tongues. I was fond of the Bangladeshi because they treated me sometimes to a piece of white bread, which had become a rare commodity. I would run home to share it with my siblings.

Despite the apparent casualness of the setting, we lived in fear. Rumors circulated that enemies lurked in the bushes and threshold of the stadium seeking to kill us. I did not know who these enemies were or where they were coming from. We would hear gunfire in the distance and an occasional bomb. We would also see smoke rising in the distance. That was usually enough to spark the imagination of the older women, who resorted to ululating, which would frighten us all. They would cry out to us that the end was nigh and that the enemy was getting closer, at our very gates. Countless times I asked my mother, "Are the soldiers coming to kill us?"

She would harshly retort, "Have you seen anyone being killed?"

I would say that I hadn't, and she would tell me to "zip it," at which I would shrink away. This kind of abruptness was typical of her character, and I never deemed it harsh. I was accustomed to all kinds of "adult" information being withheld from me.

One day, we heard that it was going to be safe to return

to our homes for a day and collect anything else that we might need. My mother decided to go. In her haste, she had forgotten to take her travel documents—that is, her passport and other papers—and was aching for a chance to retrieve our photo albums for memory's sake. Just before my father passed away, he had purchased a life insurance plan. My mother had received a settlement from the plan, some of which she kept at our home. She had not dared reveal its hiding place in the presence of the soldiers. So she wanted to retrieve that as well. She was gone for a few hours. I was scared that I might not see her again. I had insisted that I should go with her to protect her and be her bodyguard, but she had categorically refused. In her absence, I was lost in prayer for her.

Much to our relief, she returned safe and sound with some more bags of family treasures. She had found her passport and our photo albums, which would later become some of our most prized possessions. No one thought of taking memorabilia in these times. She had also found the money. She reported, however, that the house was a mess. It had been pillaged, and all our other valuables had disappeared. We were glad that we had left the house early, for had we stayed, we would have been in the way of whoever had looted our home and therefore would have been a target for them. In that chaos and absence of law enforcement, we wouldn't have survived.

News spread that the country was sinking into despair. Its citizens were drowning themselves in a sea of blood. Neighbors were turning on each other armed with machetes and other homemade weapons.

The more we heard, the more we were distressed. We knew

that the situation was terrible. We didn't dare venture out of the stadium. In spite of what we had heard, a group of people grew impatient and decided to leave the stadium secretly. Their plan was to find safe passage into refuge, and once secured, some would return to get the rest, by way of that safe passage. They left, and all we knew was that they were never heard from again. We all assumed the worst.

Scores of people kept coming into the stadium. They also had fled the massacres that were pervasive around the country. I saw that some of them were badly injured. I saw men and women with missing limbs and children bleeding, but these were of no import compared to the extreme scenes of horrific barbarity that my seven-year-old eyes would later behold.

In the midst of this turmoil, people turned to their faith for divine intervention. A general prayer was organized so that people could address God for succor. Some were starving and desperately needed relief. My mother, Aunt Jeanine, and all of us children participated in the prayer. We all convened at a designated part of the stadium. Songs of praise were sung, and prayers were lifted into the skies. After the prayer had been conducted, some people claimed that it had been revealed to them which way would lead to safety, and prophetic words were uttered. Once again we packed our belongings and left, but this time we were not privileged to have our car. The soldiers at the stadium had confiscated it and everything that was in it. All our journeying in Rwanda henceforth would be on foot.

The details have escaped my memory, but I do know that we found our way to my paternal grandparents' home in a village in the countryside. We lived there for a few days, but my mother decided that it was best to leave the country. Aunt Godelieve later told me that my mother had seen corpses in a river she had crossed. That was enough to convince her that it was time to leave. She decided that we would head to Zaire, which is now the Democratic Republic of Congo.

Chapter 3

ZAIRE, TANZANIA, ZAMBIA

On our way to Zaire, we followed dirt roads through the thick tropical forests and evergreen shrubbery. The scorching sun in the azure sky parched our lips while the dust under our feet rose to cloud our eyes and clog our nostrils. We felt the texture of dust on our tongues and rubbed our bloodshot eyes and dragged our heavy feet.

We cringed at the scenes we witnessed. My mother told us to look away, but the carnage surrounded us. Scenes of death at its worst were inevitably thrust before our infant eyes. Shot and mutilated corpses lay everywhere. Some babies still clung to the lifeless bodies of their murdered mothers. Other babies and children had been abandoned on the roadside. We were exposed to such horrors for days, until it became somehow normal. The piercing cries of children went unheeded as we walked past them. We were moved by their plight, by the desperation echoing in our ears, but no one stopped. We were not cold or heartless, but because of the burdens everyone carried, we all walked on as if it were nothing. Everyone had his or her own survival foremost in mind. Such atrocities were not enough to stop our feet as we waded through the corpses, leaving behind the buzz of flies that vibrated on our eardrums.

I have played this scene in my head a million times over and have asked myself what kind of hatred would cause a human being to brutally snatch a mother from her babe in the wake of its defenseless sobs? Or what circumstances could cause a mother to abandon her child in such times? My mind has blocked out some of these disturbing memories, but others still plague me today. My words are insufficient to convey the intensity of what we saw.

Around this time my mother's strength was put to the test. My younger brother, Angel, suddenly felt sick and could not walk a step farther. We were all exhausted from our many days' walk. My mother had been carrying all of our belongings on her back and some on her head.

She was graceful because as a child growing up she had charge over fetching the water from the river to the homestead. She would walk miles with an empty container and return with the heavy container gracefully poised on her head. Her siblings speculated that over the years this practice had stunted her growth. She was a short woman, and my sister Mary took after her in size. Nevertheless, she was always a giant in my sight.

My mother was faced with a difficult decision. If she carried Angel on her back, she would have to leave some of our bags. In that case we would be leaving the country with basically the clothes on our backs. We moved to the side of the road so as to not hinder the passage of those behind us. She put our bags down, knelt beside Angel, and tended to his feet.

We found ourselves being spectators of the exodus, like those abandoned children on the roadsides watching the slow snake-like trail of refugees. Almost all the people looked alike, carrying all their belongings on their heads and on their backs. We watched as one by one they meandered down the dirt road and disappeared behind the clustered trees and green thickets of the forest. My mother got to her feet and stood there thinking of her next step, but she did not have the luxury of time. We could not afford to be left behind.

Just as my mother decided to leave our bags and carry a weakened Angel, a benevolent-looking man appeared from no-where. We had not noticed him come to us.

"Do you need any help?" he asked. My mother explained that Angel could not walk anymore; his little feet were worn out, and he was sick.

"I'll carry him on my back," he said. He took Angel and swung him onto his back, and we resumed our journey. My mother and this kind man struck up a conversation. We were able to learn that he was from neighboring Zaire. He had been working in Rwanda but was now returning to his country. He was a godsend and proved to be unquestionably dependable. I have often reflected on the irony of the encounter. We were fleeing a country where neighbors and compatriots were slaying each other, and yet a foreigner who didn't know us was helping us.

In the next few days we crossed the border into Zaire and headed to a refugee camp. The night after crossing the border, we laid our heads on cobblestones in the middle of nowhere. We had not found a better place to make camp. Zaire was a relatively peaceful country at the time, though there were rumors of rebels lurking in the jungle. In other words, we remained relatively safe.

Scores of souls did not make it to this camp, and a large number did not make it out again. Many souls suffered from exhaustion and collapsed to be trampled underfoot. Multitudes languished in the forests and struggled to survive on an herbivorous diet. Others refused to accept the situation and vowed that nothing would move them from the homes of their forefathers. This was the case with my maternal grandmother. She was fortunate to outlive the war: many people were murdered in their own homes, and others became murderers just to stay alive.

The most tragically affected, however, were the abandoned children who had no one to give them instructions. I have often asked myself what I would have done. Four, five, six years old—I look down, I see my dead mother. I look up, I see unfamiliar, unwelcoming faces stricken with pain, betraying physical and mental fatigue. What do I do? Do I follow the unfamiliar faces, or do I stay to waste away by the side of my lifeless mother?

After our night in the camp, my mother knew that we needed to leave that place, and for such an endeavor we needed money. Hundreds were dying as poor sanitary conditions brought on the rampant rage of cholera. We had no clean drinking water and no toilets. It was only a matter of time before one of us caught something that would quickly be transmitted to the rest and extinguish the little life we had left in us.

I do not know if it was because my mother had tremendous faith in people or had simply run out of options, but she gave the kind man from Zaire all our Rwandan money to exchange it. We had managed to smuggle it out of the country and past the military checkpoints. My mother had hidden it on us, her children. The soldiers had not bothered to frisk the very young ones. The kind man needed to go to a nearby town to find money changers. He left with every promise that he would return as soon as time would permit. We then remained to fend for ourselves. My mother was under constant pressure in these times. Questions without answers were always breathing down her neck.

"How do I feed my children?" she agonized. "I have given that man all our money. Will he ever return?" She battled to keep us alive, for she was resolved to ensure our survival. We still depended on her.

The man was gone for a few days. In an amazing display of integrity, he returned with the currency we needed, some bread, and clean drinking water. He found us weakened and emaciated. He explained to us how he had been hustled by the soldiers. This had delayed his return. We were happy and relieved to leave the camp. It had become a haven of death because of disease. We had spent most of our time there lying down, overwhelmed by both hunger and fatigue. With what was left of our strength, we ventured out into Zaire, bribing our way past barricades and roadblocks and surviving on the good graces of the Zairean people we met on our way. My mother had found out somehow that her older sister Godelieve lived in one of the cities in Zaire. We found our way there.

For whatever reason, we did not stay with my aunt Godelieve for very long. My mother had decided to head south. We were not happy to leave. We had grown accustomed to the company of our family. Aunt Godelieve says that Angel threw quite the fit when we left. Our cousins Amaryllis, Penelope, Iphigenie, and Achille (children of another older sister of my mother's who had passed away) accompanied us. They must have all been in their twenties. My mother's adventurous disposition appealed to them. As for my aunt Godelieve, she later found her way to Kenya with my uncle Felicien, where they struggled for a few years in poverty until they accumulated the resources to emigrate to Europe.

From Zaire we traveled to Tanzania by ferry and then on to Dar es Salaam, on the east coast of Tanzania. In Tanzania, we were able to secure a room in a lodge. It was a square structure with an open courtyard. In this setting, I met a fascinating man who was in a wheelchair. He was by far the most muscular man I had ever seen. He was the lodge's laundryman, and since laundry was done manually, I enjoyed watching him at work. He would roll up his sleeves and grind mountains of clothing together in a huge metal tub. As he did so, his muscles would flex, and I would watch in wonder at how a man could be that toned. I became good friends with him. He taught me Swahili and revealed the secret to his physique—it was the mountains of dirty laundry he had to wrestle with every day. I decided that my career when I grew up would be that of a laundryman.

The Tanzanians boasted an exquisite cuisine. They had a simple dish that I grew particularly fond of. It was an omelet mixed with fries. Just watching a skilled cook bring it together was fascinating. There was not a moment that I was not pressing my mother for money so I could go treat myself to it. Hunger in these days was our persistent companion, but my mother managed to keep us alive.

After a short stay, my mother decided it was time to pick up and leave. She had heard that refugees were being well received in Zimbabwe. Once again, we were sad to leave. Our cousins did not continue the whole journey with us. They opted to go to Mozambique. I was sad to bid farewell to my good friend and mentor, the laundryman in the wheelchair.

We boarded a train for Zambia. I remember the ride being long, extending over two days. When we reached Zambia, we knew no one. We spent the night outside a gas station. We were able to find some cardboard boxes that sheltered us as we huddled together through the night. The following day, we boarded a bus for Harare, the capital of Zimbabwe. Little did I know that it would be my home for the next eight years, the longest I have lived in any one country.

Chapter 4

ZIMBABWE

In 1994, Zimbabwe was one of the most prosperous nations in Africa, nicknamed the "breadbasket of Africa." Zimbabwe had been colonized by the British. It was formerly Southern Rhodesia, named after Cecil Rhodes, whose dream was to expand the British Empire across the whole of Africa. In 1980, Zimbabwe won its independence after a successful military campaign against the oppressive regime of Ian Smith. From then President Robert Mugabe led the country through a period of reconciliation between the Africans and the British oppressors. At the time, the country was economically and politically stable. Mugabe had not fully revealed his dictatorial tendencies.

We arrived in Zimbabwe at night. The bus ride from Zambia had been smooth. I was used to bumpy dirt roads, so the macadamized roads of Harare impressed me. I was fascinated by the many lights that illuminated the great city. There were skyscrapers, neon-lit hotel signs, grand houses, and rows of trees in the middle of the boulevards. Perhaps the contrast between the panorama of the savannah that we had traversed for most of the bus ride and the bright lights and bustle of the city magnified my fascination for this place. This city looked futuristic, and I had never seen anything like it.

That night and the following few days we stayed at an inn while my mother asked around to find the refugee center. Once she located it, we left the inn and boarded a *kombi*, a van used as a means of public transportation, similar to a South American jitney. As we drove through Harare to the refugee center, I saw school-going children. They looked peculiar to me. Surprisingly, they were wearing ties with their uniforms. Until then I had always thought that wearing a tie was a purely grown-up practice. I stared in amusement as we drove past groups of students and individuals on their way to school. I longed to be back in a classroom. Since we had left Rwanda, I had not had the chance to attend school. I wanted to be with other children my age and learn.

The name of the refugee center was the Transit Center. It was located in a southern suburb of Harare named Waterfalls. We got off the *kombi* with our bags and walked to the Transit Center entrance which was barricaded, with guards at the gate. We stated our purpose for being there, and they let us in. We walked down a winding dirt road to report to the office at the end of the dirt road. There we were well received and granted asylum.

We were assigned a green tent and given some local food. This was ground corn, *hupfu* in the language of the Shonas of Zimbabwe. *Hupfu* is boiled in water and stirred with a wooden cooking stick until it hardens to form *sadza,* also referred to as

John, age nine; Mary Yvette, age seven; and Angel, age six;
with their mother, Thérèse, in Waterfalls, Harare, Zimbabwe, 1995.

"mealie meal." *Sadza* is the Zimbabwean staple food. My mother could only guess at how to prepare it, but she assumed that it would not be dissimilar from her native *ubugari*, which is prepared in the same way as *sadza* but is made from ground cassava. We gathered all our belongings and set them up in our green tent. It would be our home for some months.

My memory has long been deprived of the exact constitution of the Transit Center. What I remember pertains to the sheer size of it. It truly was grand, with acres of land, woods, gardens, a clinic, a small school, offices, playgrounds, and such. There was a small Rwandan community already settled in the Transit Center. We quickly made friends. My mother also made excellent friends, some of whom would become like sisters to her. Even today I address them as my aunts. Indeed, in Africa we say,

"It takes a village to raise a child," so anyone who befriends your family becomes an aunt or uncle. Angel and Mary found friends their age to play with. I made friends with children my age but always preferred the company of the adults. I found the topics they discussed, such as politics and history, very interesting.

It seemed that we were ready for a fresh start, ready to forget the lives we had led before. Reminiscence brought only grief. We had been given a chance to start over, to bury the painful memories of what we had seen and endured. Who would have thought that our lives would change so drastically and so quickly? We had gone from being wealthy citizens to being the poorest of refugees. In such a world, how much security is there in our current circumstances? Indeed, to paraphrase the words of Job of old, the Lord had given, and the Lord had taken away.

The Transit Center was home to many refugees from other countries in Africa. In addition to Rwandans, I distinctly remember people from Zaire, Somalia, Sudan, and Burundi all clustered together in this refugee camp. Other countries might have been represented, but I am unsure. These different cultures converged, and I was fascinated by anything that was foreign to me. A boy from Zaire taught me how to dance to the beat of his *djembe,* a particular type of African drum. I basked in the diversity and enjoyed it.

I particularly appreciated the Zaireans for their vibrant worship sessions. A large white tent had been erected to that end. On some days, I would attend these sessions, and the energy emanating from them was contagious. They had *djembes* and other types of rustic musical instruments being played to their limit. They sang, danced, chanted, and preached in their native

Lingala or Swahili. They prayed out loud, each voice constrained only by the petitioner's audacity. This was their mode of prayer. They fervently expressed gratitude for having been spared from whatever foes they had fled. Whenever the music played, I found my place at the front of the congregation and performed the dances my little friend from Zaire had taught me.

Being in a different country meant learning a different language. When I first heard Shona, the language of the Shonas of Zimbabwe, I fell in love with it. I loved the musicality of it and the vivid rawness of its texture to the ear. Some Zimbabwean construction workers in the Transit Center were my first instructors. They were building what would be the first batch of rooms for those who had lived in tents long enough to qualify for more permanent accommodations. Every day I ran to the construction site to find my Shona tutors. They always seemed to have many new words to teach me. They delighted in our informal lessons. Of course, as you might guess, they also taught me all the obscene vocabulary they could remember.

In due time we children learned that we would be starting school again. We were going to attend a local school called Frank Johnson Primary School, which we nicknamed *Farai Jongwe* (the Shona equivalent of "Frank Johnson"), much to our glee. I was going to start in the second grade at age eight. This was horrendous news for me. I was too old to be in the second grade. I dreaded the thought of being with younger children and felt that I was smart enough to be with children my age, but I didn't speak Shona well and didn't speak English at all. Because the British had colonized Zimbabwe, English was the language of instruction in their schools.

We presented ourselves for the first day of school, and I knew immediately that my age would not be the only conspicuous issue. All of the other students were wearing uniforms. None of the refugee children had uniforms; we couldn't afford them. From the first day we were branded as "the refugees who did not have uniforms." We felt like the circus was in town and we were the main attraction. This was difficult for all of us but for me in particular because I didn't have a thick skin. Nothing in my earlier life had prepared me for such treatment, and my feelings were constantly being hurt by comments about me or my family's situation.

In one of our bags, my mother had packed two of my late father's suits. She sold them to a local Zimbabwean man and with the money bought us some uniforms. When we paraded into Frank Johnson Primary School wearing our brand-new school uniforms for the first time, it was like the event of the century. My teacher was so impressed that she asked me to stand up in class so that everyone could take a good look.

The taunting I endured early in school would later institute feelings of inferiority because of what I was in this and every other country that was not my own. I resorted to denying where I was from. Often I was marginalized and ridiculed because of the accent that I could not rid myself of when I tried to speak Shona or English. Most of the children would not let me play with them. Nonetheless, I liked school and in time, some children became my friends. Ironically—and regrettably—I joined in teasing other refugee children. I would say, pointing to them, "Those over there are refugees, and they live in green tents." By then we had moved out of our tent and had been granted a room. It's a sad fact that a common human trait is to be harshest with those who share our weaknesses. One would think that we would be more understanding after having walked down the same path, but we find, sadly, the recovering alcoholic being overly critical of the occasional drinker.

□

One of my favorite experiences of attending school was the weekly general meeting. The entire student body and teachers would assemble in the school cultural hall. The students sat on the wooden floor and the teachers on chairs. We started our meetings by singing the Zimbabwean national anthem. When I first heard the lyrics, I was amused. At that time, Shona still sounded peculiar to me. Until we refugee children knew the words by heart, we spent a great portion of our time practicing it and parodying it. When we finally knew how to sing it, we did so with our little chests swelling with pride. What a wonderful feeling it was to finally be able to participate without making any errors. My favorite part was the last verse, which went something like this:

> *Mwari ropafadzai nyika yeZimbabwe*
> *Nyika yamadzitateguru edu tose;*
> *Kubva Zambezi kusvika Limpopo,*
> *Navatungamiri vave nenduramo;*
> *Ngaikomborerwe nyika yeZimbabwe.*

In essence the verse was asking God to bless Zimbabwe and its leaders, the country of "all of our ancestors," from the Limpopo to the Zambezi rivers.

After singing the national anthem, we closed our eyes and bowed our heads in prayer. Once in class a student asked our teacher why we closed our eyes when we prayed.

"Because when you pray, angels come down from heaven to minister to you. They don't want to be seen so you have to close your eyes," she replied. I thought of that and decided I wanted to catch a glimpse of an angel and see what they looked like. So one time when the prayer was being offered, I quickly opened my eyes and raised my head to look around. Much to my surprise I saw . . . no angels, only my fellow students' heads bowed as usual. That would not be the last time that my teachers disappointed me.

After the prayer in our meeting, the headmaster would address us on a particular topic. The most popular one was AIDS. He would tell us that AIDS was that one thing we had to avoid at all costs. He described it as the scariest impairment to a person's body. In Zimbabwe, AIDS is a serious problem. For many years in the schools that I attended, our general assemblies were animated by awareness campaigns. Most of the time what the headmaster said was gibberish, however, because no one ever bothered to explain to us students how one could actually contract AIDS.

■

By the time I was nine, I was almost proficient in Shona. I had advanced in my learning of English at school, and I understood it well enough. So my confidence was starting to emerge. I thought I was smarter than everyone else and became an avid player of checkers. I became so skilled at it that as a nine-year-old

I would challenge the adult men. I would beat them without much effort, and they would ungraciously say that I had been lucky and had not planned my moves at all. People started referring to me as the kid who liked to play checkers.

Young boys who think themselves smart have a way of getting in trouble. I was quite a mischievous boy and often found occasion to get into enough trouble to get disciplined by my mother with the classic wooden cooking spoon (*mugoti* in Shona).

My familial chore at this time was going to the store to purchase groceries at the Cheviot Center, a shopping center composed of a few stores located directly across the road from the Transit Center gates. Aside from the general stores, other vendors sold farm produce under corrugated iron shacks that enclosed their merchandise. I loathed going to the general store because I would be seen by my school peers buying paraffin (or kerosene) for our stove. A paraffin stove was a small, portable, round device that used paraffin for fuel and stood about a little over a foot in height. All our meals were prepared on that device. Having a paraffin stove marked one as a refugee, and that was not all. I had to use a *chibuku* container (*chibuku* is a traditional Zimbabwean beer) to carry the paraffin home. Having to buy paraffin and having to carry it in a beer container past my peers was humiliating.

To retaliate for my humiliation, I would steal my mother's change and play table soccer—foosball—with other children at the Cheviot Center. Because she was an accountant by profession, it was not long before my mother discovered my treachery and disciplined me with her unfailing wooden spoon, the *mugoti*.

My mischief did not end there. I was prone to exaggeration, and I applied it to every story I told. Once, my sister Mary was out playing with the other children. She accidentally fell on the back of her head and received a slight cut that caused minor bleeding. As soon as I saw one drop of blood, I ran to my mother. Panting heavily, I told her that Mary had just had a terrible accident and that her whole head had been cut in two and her brain was hanging out. Oh, my poor mother and the anxieties I caused her!

Although a strict disciplinarian, my mother was also a wise teacher and prone to a little exaggeration herself. At the Transit Center, we had public toilets and showers. My mother disliked taking showers there, even discreetly, and so preferred sponge baths. She would lock herself in our room and give herself a sponge bath, after which Mary, Angel, and I were allowed back in the room. One day when she was dressing after a bath, I noticed a big vertical scar that ran down her stomach. Instinctively I asked her, "Mama, where do babies come from?" She looked at me and saw me staring at her scar. She sat me down and said, "You see, babies grow inside your tummy, and when they are ready to be born, the belly automatically opens itself and they come out. Then it closes itself again."

"Does it hurt?" I asked.

"Just a little bit," she replied. It made perfect sense. However, when I learned the truth from my biology teachers, I was not too thrilled with them. It has been my experience that profound, mind-altering truths, when revealed prematurely, are nothing but a headache to the one who receives them.

As you might imagine, my mother struggled to make

ends meet. The aid we received from the United Nations High Commission for Refugees (UNHCR) was scarcely enough to cover our needs. School fees were a particular challenge to her. Being an industrious woman, she planted and tended a small vegetable garden. We were then able to sell the produce as the vendors did at the Cheviot Center. I set up a wooden table covered with old newspapers on the dirt road that led to the Transit Center entrance and displayed the vegetables on it. This business venture of ours failed fairly quickly, mostly because our entire clientele were refugees. I was the vendor, and most of my customers knew my mother and had become friends with her. They bought our vegetables on credit, promising to pay later, but later was always a day away. I was not bold enough to refuse to deliver except upon payment. We abandoned this business soon enough. My mother's next project was a chicken run she oversaw. She was in charge of raising the chicks to chickens and also gathering their eggs. It was a matter of common knowledge that my mother's chickens looked best and were the healthiest. Somehow we were able to live off the revenue generated by that project.

◨

As was customary for refugees, in due time we moved out of the Transit Center. Its purpose was to allow refugees to stand solidly on their feet before venturing out on their own. We rented a room in the home of a Zimbabwean family. Their home was a fifteen-minute walk from the Transit Center. I went to school in the mornings and then to the Transit Center in the afternoon, where our chicken run was located, and then I would also work in the garden. We were still growing our own vegetables.

My mother was usually absent all day and returned home in the evenings, by which time I would have dinner cooked. She would reward me with her angelic smile and exaggerated compliments on the quality of the meal I'd prepared.

On some evenings she failed to conceal her sadness from me when she returned home, although she attempted to. I did not understand what was bothering my mother, but I knew that whatever it was, I could not help her. I was almost ten years old and had been compelled to mature quickly. I was the man of the house. To cheer her up, I applied myself more diligently to my schoolwork. That was one way I knew that would lift her spirits. Though I did not know at the time the cause of her unhappiness, my mother knew she was afflicted with a problem beyond her control.

I also suppose that she felt that life was not advancing fast enough for her. She was not where she wanted to be and felt hindered by circumstance. In light of our predicament, she was doing well for herself and her children. But she did not give herself enough credit. I also imagine that she was lonely. Many a time I caught her stealing a glance at her wedding pictures. All of the friends she associated with at the Transit Center had survived their struggles alongside their husbands, but she was there alone with no one to help her pull the weight. I believe that all she needed once in a while was a break, but she never got one.

At the height of her struggles, my mother contracted hepatoma, an aggressive and deadly cancer. The poor woman practically worked herself to death. The combination of severe

John's parents, Jean-Baptiste and Thérèse,
at their wedding, Rwanda, 1986.

emotional and mental strain as well as malnutrition finally took its toll on her. She was admitted to the Transit Center clinic, and my siblings and I returned there to live. For a few weeks we did not see her. One of my mother's closest friends, whom we knew as Aunt Christine, took care of us. Not long after, another of my mother's friends, Aunt Annonciata, sent her eldest daughter, Claudine, to live with us.

After those few weeks, I learned that my mother had been moved to another clinic, not far from the Transit Center. Aunt Annonciata told me that I needed to go see her and that it would cheer her up. A Catholic priest was also going to accompany me to give my mother a blessing. I had just won some academic medals at school for my ability as a student. I had placed first, not only in my class but also in my whole grade. I was sure that my medals would make her happy. The first time I had brought her my report card had been in our early days in Zimbabwe. I didn't speak any of the languages, so I had not done well in school. This time, however, was different.

We arrived at the care facility where she was being treated. We stated the purpose of our visit to the receptionist, who gave me a long sad look when she learnt I was my mother's son. She ushered us into the waiting room and was dramatically courteous and offered me all kinds of treats.

Then they brought out my mother, and when I saw her, I stood transfixed to the floor. My heart pounded in my ears and tears welled up in my eyes. My mother was barely recognizable. She was in a wheelchair; her light-complexioned face was now a dark, skeletal visage. She had dark rings under her eyes, and her head drooped forward as if her neck could barely support it. A shawl concealed her completely bald head. A small portion of her lower legs was visible; they had swollen to the size of tree trunks.

Tears streamed down my face; I was afraid to approach her. The receptionist called out to me, "That's your mother. Go to her."

I hesitated and then made a few calculated steps towards her. I don't think that she had noticed me until then. She lifted her eyes up to me and made no sign of recognition. In a barely audible voice I stuttered, "Mama. . . . I . . . I . . . I brought you my medals."

She did not seem to hear me. The nurse who had brought her handed me a cup of orange juice and told me it was for my mother. I approached her and held the cup to her lips so she could drink the juice.

The priest began to conduct his blessing. My mother suddenly reacted to the priest, asking him the purpose of his visit. He told her that he had come on behalf of God to bless her. Then she asked him, "Where is He now?" and then repeated loudly, "Where is He now?" Before the priest could reply, she said, "Let Him be gone!" and she gesticulated as if shooing Him away.

I was aching to take my leave of her. My heart was heavy, beholding what had become of my mother and the anguish she was enduring. This woman was not only my mother but the sweetest of ladies there ever was. To see her in that chair, in that pain, and in that mood, was the most heart-wrenching experience I had ever undergone. The nurses took her away. The second she was out of sight, I ran home as fast as my little legs could go. I burst into our small room, got on my knees, and pleaded, "God, please take her away with You to Your home so she won't ever have to hurt anymore." Both my hands, tightly clutched together in supplication, were bathed in my warm tears. The next thing I remember was waking up to find I had been gently laid in bed. I had fainted.

Claudine was still with us, tending to all of our needs to the best of her ability. One day she said, "Yves, promise me that when she is taken away, you won't cry." Without hesitation I said, "I promise."

Everyone in the Transit Center and beyond knew she was dying. Now many years later, I know why she appeared sad on those evenings when I sensed her somber mood. I have since been informed that when she learnt that her illness was terminal, her otherwise cheerful disposition dampened, but nothing tortured her soul more than the tragedy she supposed would befall her three small soon-to-be-orphaned children. My mother blamed God for the travails she had undergone. Her mind was in agony, and her body was in excruciating pain. She wasted away, lamenting her poor children who would become orphans in a foreign country. As a devout Christian, I was distressed at the destination of her soul after death. She had forsaken God in front of me from her wheelchair. All I knew to that point had taught me that what I had seen was an unpardonable sin.

And so when I was ten years old, Mary eight, and Angel seven, I woke up on a quiet morning to find people gathered around our home. Claudine told me gently that my mother had passed away. I could also read it on people's long faces. People kept coming to our home to pay their respects because my mother was truly loved by many. Her death did not come as a surprise to me; I had been expecting it. After my father's death and the many souls I saw fall victim to the genocide, I knew death as a constant, if unwanted, part of life.

The fruit of her death was bittersweet. In my heart I wanted her to go, because I had seen her suffering and could not bear the thought that of all the people in the world, my mother had been afflicted in that manner. But as a child, I wanted her to remain with us because she was our mother. I am amazed at the faith I exhibited as a child. I was convinced that my mother was going to a better place. Sadly, the older I grew, the more doubtful I became of divine notions.

At the news of her passing, I remembered a conversation I had held with her in which she said, "You, Yves, I am hard on because you are the eldest. You will take care of Angel and Mary. You can't be acting like them."

To this day, my heart sometimes dampens in sorrow when I think of the burdens I had to bear in my childhood. I grieve even more over the burdens my mother had to bear: losing a husband when still so young and so in love, fending for three children through a war, living in poverty in a foreign country, wrestling with a painful disease even unto death. I recall one of the saddest conversations I ever held with another person concerning my mother. I spoke with the doctor who had been in charge of her case. I had been designated to collect her items from the care facility. "What was wrong with my mother? What did she die from, ma'am?" I asked her.

"Malnutrition," the doctor replied.

"What's *ma-noo-tee-shen*, ma'am?" I enquired.

"Mal-nu-tri-tion," she repeated, emphasizing the syllables. "It means that your mother was not eating right."

Ironically, none of us had been eating properly for years, yet we lived and she did not.

◘

The day of the funeral arrived. There was a large turnout of friends and well-wishers, most of whom were from the Rwandan community in the Transit Center. Both Angel and I wore dark suits; Mary wore a white dress. We had our mother's requiem, and I had a last chance to see her in her casket. Someone had tended to her appearance, and she looked peaceful, as if she were in deep slumber. As I stood over her casket gazing at her face, my mind raced back to the time when my father had been in this same slumber and I had tried to wake him by pulling on his big toe. I slowly stretched out my hand to touch her forehead in good-bye, right after my siblings. It was stone cold from the refrigeration.

After the farewell mass, Angel, Mary, and I were driven to the burial site in a white van provided by the UNHCR. Some men carried my mother's casket to her final resting place, and we followed the procession of mourners to the site. Father Peter Baleis, a German priest my mother had befriended, officiated at the funeral. Rwandan funeral songs were sung, led by Aunt Annonciata. Their poignant spirit weighed heavily on my grieving heart. We all stood around the burial plot and watched her casket being lowered into the earth. A man with a shovelful of earth lifted it to me, and I took some in my hands and sprinkled it on her casket. Then I walked slowly back to the van. Angel and Mary joined me. An Ethiopian lady who had become close friends with my mother rode with us, crying her heart out, ululating and overdoing the theatrics while we watched. Then somebody yelled out, "We need to get that woman out of there. She is making the kids cry."

◧

It was decided that my siblings and I would be split up. I would live with Aunt Annonciata, while Mary and Angel lived with Aunt Christine. Aunt Annonciata had six children of her own. Alice was my age, Elise was younger, and the rest—Assumpta, Immaculée, Eric, and Claudine—were older. They were family to us, because we had known each other from the time we had come to the Transit Center. Since Eric was two years older than me, he became my big brother.

Aunt Christine, with whom Mary and Angel went to live, had three children of her own: her daughter Maggie was Mary's age; her son, Fils, was Angel's age; and her daughter Cristella was the youngest. It had been decided that since Mary and Angel were inseparable it would be best to keep them together. Some days into that arrangement, both families noticed signs of depression and withdrawal in us and decided it was better for us to be together in one family. So I went to join my siblings with my other aunt, Christine. Both families showed us unbelievable compassion. I do not think that we felt any different from their other children. We felt at home.

Visiting other parts of the world has shown me how blessed we were to be in the company of kind people who would take us into their homes and treat us as their own children when we were not even related by blood. In Europe and America, I have witnessed people—even sons and daughters—who could not stand to live with those they were related to.

I continued at Frank Johnson Primary School, but after my mother's death, I did not shine as I had before. I did not have her there to please anymore.

Chapter 5

EMERALD HILL

One day my aunt Christine told us that we were to attend boarding school. She explained that we would be "going to school and returning home to the nuns." I was glad; it seemed as though everyone at Frank Johnson Primary School was well-acquainted with our recent misfortune, so I rejoiced in our imminent departure. I was disappointed, however, to learn that it would be only my siblings and me who would be subject to such an outcome. I had not imagined that my aunt's children would not join us. We said our good-byes and loaded our bags onto the white van that, once again, had been provided by the U.N. to facilitate our relocation. We were driven through Harare, heading north until we arrived in a neat-looking neighborhood. Our destination was a large compound perched on the apex of a green hill called, appropriately, Emerald Hill.

We pulled up to a gate manned by a security guard at the very end of a street named Dorset Road. The driver had a brief exchange with the guard and, at our driver's explanation of our situation, the guard opened the gate and bade us enter. We entered the driveway and started a winding ascent toward a group of buildings.

The first thing that I noticed was the presence of many other children. They crowded in toward our van, peering inside to see who we were. When the van stopped, we all stepped off and stood there feeling, and probably looking, unsure of ourselves. A woman who had come out to welcome us invited us to follow her. She led us to the head nun's office in the building before us.

The head nun's name was Sister Gabriel Flender. She was white, a Dominican nun from Germany. She was tall and had an engaging smile and a wise, middle-aged face behind her spectacles. She talked with my aunt about us, and after a lengthy conversation, my aunt stood up to leave. Before she did, she assured us that we would see her soon. She also admonished us to be on our best behavior. Then she got back in the van and disappeared around the corner. We were sad to see her leave. Although I had found my previous circumstances at Frank Johnson Primary School awkward, this new situation filled me with dread.

And so we were left to ourselves in this boarding school, home to about a hundred children, ranging in age from three to nineteen. The first thing we learned was that this was not a boarding school at all. It was an orphanage, mostly for AIDS orphans. That seemed to explain why my aunt's children had not come with us.

Soon, however, we learned the actual reason: my aunt Christine, who had brought us to Emerald Hill, had won the green-card lottery and left for the United States. When my

John, age ten, at the Emerald Hill Children's Home in Zimbabwe.

mother had still been in good health, she and Christine had submitted green-card applications to the U.S. embassy. Christine had, of course, mentioned only her three children on her application. When Christine received her green card after my mother's death, it became impossible for her to be our legal guardian, even though my mother had designated Christine and Annonciata in her will as our foster parents. Later I learnt that she tried everything within her means to take us with her, but the U.S. embassy would not allow it. She was advised to leave us in Zimbabwe and claim us once she arrived in America. In accordance with this counsel she decided to leave us there, believing that it would not be long before we were reunited. She told Sister Gabriel to watch over us for a little while.

◙

The Emerald Hill orphanage was composed of several buildings, the first being the one we had been ushered into that first day. Adjacent to it was a cottage for visiting European volunteers who donated their time and service at the orphanage. Opposite the cottage was the convent for the Dominican sisters. It was a two-story building with many windows, one for each of the sisters' rooms. There was a chapel inside this building. It was also connected to the dining room for the students of the Emerald Hill School for the Deaf. As the name suggests, there was also as part of the compound a school for deaf children. Though we shared the premises, we did not mingle with them.

At Emerald Hill we were assigned to a dormitory. Each dormitory housed approximately fourteen children and was segregated by gender, with some older children and some younger. The boys' dormitories were located on the first floor. The girls were on the second. The senior girls, aged thirteen to eighteen, lived at the end of the hall of the first floor, down some stairs. They had their own courtyard and a matron to supervise them. The senior girls each shared a room with another girl. The choice and assignment of roommates among the senior girls was a matter of common dispute.

Sister Gabriel's office was located on the first floor as well, adjacent to the boys' dormitories. Next to Sister Gabriel's office was an office occupied by a Zimbabwean social worker, Mrs. Wasterfalls. The infirmary was opposite Mrs. Wasterfalls' office; we referred to it as the sick room. Sister Gabriel's room was connected to the infirmary and stood opposite one of the dormitories.

At night we were to strictly observe total silence lest we wake up Sister Gabriel. We were all terrified of her. She was as tough as nails and was known to physically discipline a rowdy child on occasion. The children at the orphanage had given her a nickname, "Gaba," but saying it in her presence was enough to rob her of her composure—she firmly disliked the term. If another child was bothering you and you found yourself unable to defend yourself, all you had to do was threaten to tell Gaba, and that was usually enough to inspire the perpetrator to stop.

Both the boys and girls had matrons who oversaw the dormitories. They rotated shifts, so we did not always have the same matron. We called them *sisi*, which means "sister" in Shona. They were all Zimbabwean ladies, and all spoke Shona; some of them also spoke Ndebele, the other dialect spoken in Zimbabwe. Some were stricter than others, and naturally every child had his or her favorite. Mine was Sisi Alfa, a heavyset, middle-aged African woman with a kind face. I like to believe that I was her favorite orphan as well, because she went to great lengths to give me advice about how I should conduct myself in order to be happy at the orphanage and in life generally.

Our most thrilling sport as children was to catch the matrons making a grammatical or pronunciation error when speaking English. Because we felt that they terrorized us at times, we found a great deal of pleasure in catching them when their English-speaking proficiency was less than it ought to have been. Being able to speak English properly in a country that was familiar with it only by adoption was not an inconsequential matter. If you made a grammatical or pronunciation error, everyone would jump on the bandwagon to humiliate you. Ironically enough, the least proficient were usually the first to launch the attack. In those humiliating moments, you would hear someone say, "*Usazvinetse shamwari, chakauya nengarava.*" This meant, "Don't trouble yourself, good friend. It came on a ship," referring to the white people arriving centuries prior in ships and bringing with them the English language. The better the English you spoke, the more you were respected as a well-cultivated child. If you became adept, however, you were labeled as a snob. You would then be nicknamed "the nose brigade," because those who attempted to speak with a Western accent were nasal in their pronunciation.

◘

We observed a set schedule at Emerald Hill. We were roused from sleep around 6:00 A.M. We would make our beds, the older children helping the very young ones. Then we showered under the watchful eyes of the matron in charge, who was there to allocate the amount of soap to be used. The older boys showered in separate shower rooms and were afforded a bar of soap of their own. When you attained the age of showering separately, beyond the matron's scrutiny, you knew you were living the life.

After showering, we dressed for school. Our school uniforms were khaki shorts and shirt, black-and-blue-striped tie, knee-length gray socks, and brown shoes. We would then go to the dining room that was located next to the boys' dressing rooms. We took our meals together as a family. Sister Gabriel was sometimes present to lead us in prayer, after which we wolfed down our meals. We had assigned seats in the dining room. Each table was composed of six children, including an appointed table leader, usually a senior girl. She was responsible for fetching the food from the kitchen counter. It would have been chaos if we had observed an every-man-for-himself policy. Mealtimes were always animated by lively conversation and general camaraderie.

The most spectacular part of our meals was when someone wanted a second serving of food. You had to take your plate, walk up to the kitchen counter under the scrutiny of all those present, and borrow Oliver Twist's line, "May I have some more?" When the kitchen staff was in a good mood, they indulged you. But if one of them happened to be in an ill humor on that particular day—which was usually the case—you would be refused. You then had to walk back to your seat with your empty plate in hand. At the climax of that moment of shame, everyone would hiss, "*hiiiiiiiiiiii*" to humiliate you some more. Going for seconds always required a lot of guts.

□

There was a boy who was a year older than I who had lived at Emerald Hill for a long time. I idolized him. He always wore more fashionable clothes than the rest of us and was therefore "cool." He had flair, was an excellent athlete, and spoke good English. I wanted to be just like him. This boy was allergic to pasta. He could not eat any macaroni or spaghetti when those were on the menu. So when we did have them, the kitchen staff would give him the ground beef that accompanied the pasta and some bread. He ate different food from everybody else, and we thought that it was so cool. I was determined to be exactly like him, so I would be considered cool like him. I declared that I was allergic to pasta too. The only problem was that pasta was my favorite dish. For many years I regrettably partook of the miserable bread and ground beef, and no one thought that I was particularly cooler. There may have been a hint or two made in that regard, but nothing dramatically rewarding was ever advanced to my credit. It was a painful lesson: I was better off being the very best version of myself than a dreadful copy of someone else.

After our breakfast we would board the van to go to school. All the children from Emerald Hill were driven to school in a big white van that was labeled "Emerald Hill School for the Deaf." The school for the deaf had put it at our disposal for our daily commute to school.

My new school was Avondale Primary. I would be starting in the fourth grade. On my first day, I was assigned to sit next to a pretty white girl named Robyn. She was awfully nice to me and let me borrow some of her school supplies when I was in need. I made some good friends; one girl in particular, Tatenda Kumire, would share her lunch with me. There was also a teacher, Mrs. Nhago, who took a particular interest in my siblings and me. We went to see her during our lunch break sometimes. She usually asked us if there was anything we needed. She would also enquire after our well-being and livelihood. Then she would send us off with some money and encouraging words. I never found out how she knew us or how she started caring about our welfare; however, that was not the only time someone would take a similar interest in us.

We stayed in school until the early afternoon. We were then picked up from school and went back to Emerald Hill for lunch. Some children had to return to school for sports activities. The rest would stay at Emerald Hill and study. In the late afternoon we were allowed to play. We had all kinds of sports activities and fun games. The boys enjoyed soccer on the green field in front of the main building.

The girls preferred a game we called "rounders." It was a simple game played on a rectangular perimeter. Each of the four corners of the rectangle represented a home base. The gist of the

John, age eleven, in Zimbabwe, 1997.

game was to get through all four bases without being hit by the ball. Two players on the opposing team stood between the second and the third base, throwing the ball to each other back and forth while you tried to make a dash for it to the next base. The trick was to dodge the ball when it was thrown at you, so that it would go beyond the perimeters. When your opponents rushed to retrieve it, you would run from base to base, earning points. We all enjoyed this game, and it drew a large crowd.

In the evenings, we assembled together in the dining room for dinner. After dinner we went back to our studies, after which we retired to our dormitories for the night.

Weekends were different. We did not attend school but had chores to perform. We had more time to play, and it was the only time that we could watch television. We had choir practice on Saturdays for church the following day. The most coveted assignment was that of drummer. Everyone wanted to be a drummer, and a lot of days were spent practicing just to be considered for the celebrated team of drummers. On Sundays, we had mass and usually a delicious lunch. We were allowed to watch movies in the afternoon and enjoy a relaxing day.

◘

School holidays were the most anticipated season of the school year. We had three months of school and then a month's holiday throughout the whole year. I can still remember being driven back home on the very last day of school. The atmosphere was electrifying with all the children singing the whole way back at the top of their voices:

> *Gore rapera, toenda kunozorora,*
> *Gore rapera, toenda kunozorora,*
> *Good-bye my teacher,*
> *Toenda kunozorora.*

It meant "the year is over, we are going to rest, good-bye, my teacher, we are going to rest." It was a real anthem, harmonized by the blend of our little African voices.

◘

No sooner had my aunt Christine settled in the United States than she immediately dedicated herself to initiating an adoption procedure for us, to enable our immigration there in the hope of a reunion. She wrote a letter apologizing to us for the manner in which our placement in the orphanage had been conducted. She explained to us why her departure had necessitated the utmost discretion lest some well-known individuals with ill will toward her foil her fragile plans.

She sought and acquired the legal documents that were required to meet the demands of the adoption. The last remaining obstacle was to obtain custody of us. After my mother's death, custody was transferred to the German priest she had befriended, Father Peter Baleis. Father Baleis had a different interpretation of the circumstances regarding Aunt Christine's departure to the United States and our placement in the orphanage. He disapproved of the plan for her to adopt us and vowed never to place us in her custody. His opposition rendered her efforts futile.

I took the news terribly. I could hardly have taken it any worse—I had been mentally building up to the possibility of going to America. We were all fond of our aunt and held her and her children in high esteem. In addition, I had heard all sorts of marvelous legends about America. The one that impressed me the most was that America was a land of promise, a country where you could go with just the shirt on your back and emerge a millionaire. This tale inspired me and was the sweetest music to my ears. I was convinced that all I needed was an opportunity, and with that opportunity I could make a name for myself and provide a better life for my siblings. I did not see an abundance of options in that orphanage in Zimbabwe. The moment I heard about the American dream, I fell deeply in love with America and vowed that one day I would go there to realize my dream.

At about the same time, my aunt Annonciata had an opportunity to emigrate from Zimbabwe to the Netherlands. She was the last person remaining who had been close to our mother. In those initial months at the orphanage, she sent her eldest daughter, Claudine, to fetch us on long weekends. We rode public transportation all the way across town to Waterfalls, where Annonciata still resided. These were the best of times. I spent my days roaming around with her son, Eric, both of us up to no particular good, chasing girls and playing pranks on the others. On one occasion, we thought it was funny to urinate in a container that was usually used to store drinking water. Soon one of my aunt's daughters, Immaculée, suffered the consequences of our prank. She drank from the container, much to her chagrin when she tasted the foul contents. When my aunt found out, she was furious and fervently reprimanded us, mostly Eric, however, for he was older.

When Aunt Annonciata left Zimbabwe, we felt very alone. She stayed in touch with us, writing us letters, sending us birthday cards, calling us at the orphanage, and sometimes even sending us money. Nevertheless, the reality of the situation was that all we had was each other. Her departure became a greater incentive for my drive to leave Zimbabwe. I tried to imagine how on earth I could go to America without Father Baleis's approval. No matter how vigorously I exerted my mind, I could not devise a good enough plan by solitary effort. So I watched American movies instead, just to feel close to my dream. I compared the lives that I saw depicted in the movies with the one that I led and observed a considerable contrast. I promised myself that I would never stop trying to get to America somehow, someday, no matter what the cost.

This was the genesis of my quest to make my lofty dream come true. In the following years, I learned what it would take to attain such a goal and grew to appreciate the substance of which dreams are made. The first principle I learned was that when you have a big dream, those who do not share your dream will oppose you. Enemies suddenly spring forth with weapons of sophistication against you. Psychological warfare ensues, your only arsenal the fire that burns so passionately in your chest. When that fire is constantly fed, it can spread to consume everything in its way. But most of the time, one or two defeats will set the fire to sputtering and you surrender, saying to yourself that it was a crazy idea in the first place. The passion that was once so vibrant slowly finds extinction, and you join the ranks of general society again to watch with resentment those who deserve to win winning. I was twelve years old, and it seemed that at that age and at that time, no one took me seriously. I was left with my ambition to kick against a wall I could not scale.

◨

Months went by without a change in circumstance, and then one day, Father Baleis informed me that we had an aunt living in Brussels, Belgium. She had emigrated to Belgium from a refugee camp in Kenya, obtained asylum in Belgium, and was living there as a refugee, along with her husband Felicien, my uncle. This aunt in Belgium was my aunt Godelieve, with whom we had stayed in Zaire. She had fought overwhelming odds to land in Belgium. Only those who have toiled in destitution in a third-world country and successfully escaped poverty and all its ills to secure better living conditions in Europe, America, or elsewhere can fully appreciate the enormity of this task. Because of the inherent uncertainty and risk of her undertaking, she had gone first, relying on faith alone. After her safe passage, my uncle Felicien followed, to be reunited with her. They knew what our situation was because she had been in correspondence with

Father Baleis. They felt responsible for us and decided it was up to them to get us out of Zimbabwe, so they sought to adopt us.

Many years earlier, Godelieve had basically raised my mother. My mother was the youngest of eleven children. Aunt Godelieve was about sixteen years older than my mother and had, as one of the older siblings, helped my grandmother raise my mother. After the Rwandan genocide of 1994, my grandmother was still living in her village in her old age. She told my aunt Godelieve that she would not die in peace as long as her youngest daughter's children were stuck in an orphanage in a foreign country. Therefore my aunt promised to do all in her power to rectify the situation.

When I heard of my aunt's intentions, I went to Sister Gabriel and asked her, "Is Belgium close to America?" and she replied, "It's sure closer than Zimbabwe."

That was more than enough for me. As long as it would take me closer to my dream, I was ready to pack and leave that day. Unfortunately for me, it was not that simple. Although I expected then to leave any day, my day would not come for three long years.

◘

When my aunt began the process, she approached an adoption and immigration expert for counsel. She explained what the situation was and wanted to know the best way to proceed. After hearing how complex our situation was, the expert told her, "The best thing you can do for those children is to stay in touch with them and send them money occasionally. Anything more is not possible." She was a refugee in Belgium, and the financial aid she received was scarcely enough to cover her needs. About this time, Father Baleis left Zimbabwe, and custody over us was transferred to competent Zimbabwean authorities. This further complicated our situation. It was too complex a case to be attempted by people with nonexistent resources. What does one do when told by the foremost experts that what they are attempting is simply not possible?

My aunt Godelieve is endowed with extraordinary patience. The discouraging counsel she received during her initial attempt weighed heavily on her. It did not deter her for a moment, however. After what she had survived and after what we had survived, she was convinced that nothing was impossible if she had the will. Having survived the life of a fugitive in a foreign land at her advanced age was proof enough that anything was possible. She decided to face this legal maze and challenge her Goliath.

Our biggest obstacle in that undertaking was our lack of access to some documents that were required by both the Zimbabwean and Belgian authorities. For instance, we had to produce his death certificate to prove that my father had indeed died. How on earth were we supposed to get a death certificate from the postwar government of a country we had all fled? These and many others were the challenges we faced as we set the adoption on its way.

The expert counsel that my aunt needed to consult was expensive. She did not work; my uncle did not hold a highly lucrative job at the time either. Under those circumstances, what we were doing was, as people say, building castles in Spain. In those years of my life, I was left to reflect often on why some people were born to a life of ease, never accustomed to loss or pain and continually obtaining the things they wanted in life while most others, like me, did not. Many times I was left to lament how unfair life was. It seemed that the smallest accommodations that life had afforded us were subject to opposition of some kind. Everything we had, we had had to fight for. Whatever banal privilege we enjoyed, we had a scar to show for it.

I have seen that when you settle for what you have, for the mediocre or the safe, you are shielded from much worry. But when you have a dream of a better life, in a far distant land, you are bound to become acquainted with sorrow in your attempt to attain it. Many a time I was driven to question the veracity of the optimistic dream that I had heard professed countless times and grown to passionately espouse myself. However, the closest I came to my dream in those years was when I thought my lot so dreadful that the only way to quench the raging thirst in my soul was to retire to my fantasy world to escape reality.

Chapter 6

THE DENDERES

Before my mother passed away, she befriended a lady from Mauritius who worked for the U.N. in Harare. Her name was Christine Dendere, and she was married to a Zimbabwean man, Tigere Dendere. We had visited the Denderes when my mother was alive, and they had been delighted when we spent the night. Mr. Dendere was a military man. From the day he laid his eyes upon us, he fell in love. He immediately declared us his own, and from that day he became the father figure in my life.

He was a kind and gentle man with a winning smile. He had the build of an athlete and was in his early thirties. He must have stood more than six feet tall, but back then, anyone who was significantly taller than I seemed to be of that height. He reminded me of my father. They shared the same casualness about life, so he was an easily likeable character. His wife Christine was a small, beautiful woman with an exotic look and mannerisms. When we first met them, they had two children of their own, Sheu and Schola. A third, Anna, was born after we had been acquainted for a considerable stretch of time. Their children were all younger than my youngest sibling, Angel.

Authorization from a particular governmental ministry was required for Mr. Dendere to take us to his home for the holidays. He always took the trouble to obtain it, never deterred by the formality. I was always excited about leaving the orphanage for a while and enjoying a normal family setting. He introduced us as his children, even to his own relatives. I relished hearing him claiming us as his own, but Christine was ever disposed to bring us back to reality by saying, "No, they are our little friends from Rwanda."

I loathed being associated with that country and felt Shona to my core. At this time in my life I spoke Shona fluently, without a trace of an accent. I had grown to embrace the Shona culture, and my mind had adjusted itself to a new way of life. I was ashamed of being a refugee. My mother had sensed this and assured me that there was no shame in being a refugee: even Jesus Himself had been a refugee in Egypt when his parents fled to protect Him from Herod. In the urgency of the moment, I took comfort in that practical perspective, but it wasn't ever long before her words were swept away like chaff in the wind.

When I was twelve, Mr. Dendere started teaching me how to drive. He usually allowed me to drive around the army barracks, and sometimes he and I would venture beyond the barracks. Seeing me behind the wheel was fascinating to the general public. People were shocked to see me drive because I looked exactly my age, and I had to use a cushion to see above the steering wheel. I suppose that Mr. Dendere was proud when he saw me applying the lessons he had persistently instilled in me. When he drove us back to Emerald Hill, he would stop in front of the gate and switch seats with me, and I would then drive up the hill. In that last stretch, the other children would hurry out to see me pull up to the home. I would then be the subject of interest and a little hero for a few days. When the excitement of my exploits died down, I felt robbed. I always thought that the excitement deserved to last a little longer.

For many years Mr. Dendere was my father, and I looked up to him. He made us feel like his own and cared for us. We always felt included. He was our emotional rock as well. My sister, Mary, who around that age was a tomboy, received a great deal of teasing from me about her lack of femininity. He always flew to her defense and boosted her self-esteem by reassuring her that all that mattered was that she feel comfortable with herself. Mary grew up to be a very headstrong, opinionated, and self-loving young woman, completely at peace with herself.

I recall a time when Mr. Dendere's sister was having a wedding. As the wedding preparations proceeded, the tailor who was charged with fitting us with our wedding apparel failed to measure me correctly. My suit did not fit. I was upset and sulked in solitude, not telling a soul the reason for my foul mood. I have no idea how Mr. Dendere knew, but the night before the wedding, he shook me from my sleep and presented me with a suit that I could wear the next day. I was as ecstatic as I was surprised, and to this day I am mystified at how he became aware of my discontent or of the cause of it.

Mr. Dendere trusted me, even at an early age, to run significant errands for him. I remember a time when he entrusted me

John, age thirteen, in Zimbabwe, 1999;
a picture Mr. Dendere kept in his office.

with an errand, but I was met with some trouble when I tried to execute it. He charged me to go to a different town, Mount Darwin, to fetch some papers for him. To get there, I needed to board a *kombi* for a journey of about two hours. I arrived in Mount Darwin, received the papers, and made my way back to Harare by the same mode of transport. However, the *kombi* dropped me off in an area of Harare I was unfamiliar with. I did not have a phone or any other way to ask Mr. Dendere to come and pick me up in that area. I decided to ask around for the nearest *kombi* station that would take me home. There, in unfamiliar territory, I saw two ruffian-looking men on a street corner. They wore ragged clothing, looked like they were in their thirties, and seemed to be selling shoe polish or running a shoeshine business. Their establishment consisted of a cardboard box table and two chairs—that was all. Although I would rather have avoided these two fellows, my need for directions exceeded the unease I felt. So I approached them and asked them for directions, and one of them, the smaller one, said, "Hey man, let me hook you up with a free shoeshine."

"I'm wearing sneakers," I said.

"That's okay, man, it's free!"

"Well, I just need directions," I responded.

"Don't worry, bro, I'll take you there myself," he answered. I thought to myself, *What a nice man this fellow is.* He proceeded to clean my shoes, and as soon as he was finished, he demanded fifty Zimbabwean dollars. I was confused. I reminded him that he had said it would be free.

"Man, we're in Zim—where do you get anything for free?" he shot back scornfully. I told him that I did not have any money with me. At that point he got angry and he told the bigger man, who was a frightening sight to behold, to "take care of me." The bigger man approached me in a militant fashion, and my adrenaline started pumping, my hair stood on end, and my legs shook as I tried to think quickly about what to do. I could not run. These two were older, larger, and therefore much faster than me.

The man grabbed me roughly by the collar and said, "Pay up, boy!"

In my fright I managed to stutter, "I can get the money at the *kombi* station." He paused for a moment, released his grip, and told me he would accompany me there. We headed to the *kombi* station while my mind ran wild with plans for what I would do once we reached our destination. Maybe I could just scream and say that this man was trying to hustle me and he would get scared and run away. Then I thought that people might not care, and this man, then angry, would do his worst. In a flash, a moment of intelligence graced my mind.

"Hey, man," I said, "I'm glad you're coming with me, because my father is waiting for me at the station, and I am sure he will be more than happy to give you the money once I explain to him what happened."

The man seemed a bit uneasy now, and he repeated, "Your father is gonna be there?"

"Yeah," I replied, "you don't have to worry about anything. He's a nice man and a captain in the army."

Then the man seemed mighty anxious. It was not long before he said, "You know what? Forget the money. The station is that way." He pointed me in the right direction and hastily took off.

Phew, what a relief! I was glad that I had been blessed with the words to scare this crook away. I found my way home and told the story later at the dinner table. Mr. Dendere and everyone else present were quite amused that evening.

All was not always well, however, for I did my fair share to disappoint Mr. Dendere. One time Angel and I went to get the groceries with a list his wife, Christine, had given us. It turned out that she had not given us enough money to purchase all the items on the list. I did not want to go back so I decided that I would shoplift the items I couldn't buy. I clumsily performed the deed and paid for what I could. At the exit, just as I was starting to feel safe, a hand on my shoulder stopped me and turned me around to face the security guard. She was a mountain of a lady and succeeded without much effort to frighten me to death. She inspected my bags while comparing the contents with the receipt. She noticed that some items were indeed not on the receipt. She shot me a look of disdain and shook her head. She beckoned us to follow her and ushered us into a back office.

The second we set foot behind closed doors, she slapped me

across the face. "You think you can come here and steal from me, boy? Who are your parents?" Amid my sobs, I quickly told her that Mr. Dendere was at work. She extracted his phone number from me and called to tell him what had happened. After talking to him for a while, she hung up the phone and told us that he was on his way. She showed us out and told us to wait for him. She gave us back our bags, excluding the stolen items.

When I saw Mr. Dendere's car approaching, I was terrified and tempted to take flight. He spotted us and pulled up beside us. We instinctively stepped into the car. He did not look at us or utter a single word. Because I was expecting an outburst—and probably a good beating—this was worse. I sat there agonizing over what he was thinking or what he was going to do, but he drove on toward home. We arrived there after what seemed an eternity. The silence had been terribly awkward. When we got home, Angel and I stepped out of the car, and he drove back to work. He said nothing to us about it. I was uncomfortable and avoided him for the next couple of days, but he never mentioned anything regarding the matter. I never shoplifted again.

This impressed upon my mind that my mother's corporeal methods of reproof were not the only way to discipline silliness. More important, I learnt that Mr. Dendere's chagrin at my mischief was proof of great affection, for where there is great affection you find great disappointment.

Even after my shoplifting episode, the Denderes still came to get us every holiday. Mr. Dendere was very much aware of my longing to go to Belgium and to America, and he agreed that being with my biological family would be ideal. I suspect that though he even helped us meet some of the legal requirements, he did so reluctantly. He had grown very much attached to us. The Denderes played a significant role in our lives, and for me, their friendship was the one prospect I looked forward to when I could not stand the orphanage any more.

Chapter 7

SAINT IGNATIUS COLLEGE

About two years had elapsed since my aunt had breathed life into the adoption procedure. I had made great strides in school and was in my last year at Avondale Primary School, grade seven. I was well-known as the high achiever in academics. I had also been named the deputy head prefect. This was a prestigious position, especially for a student from the orphanage. My position required that I assist the teachers in maintaining order in school.

Boys who completed primary school would leave Emerald Hill. The girls stayed to become senior girls. Boys were transferred to an all-boys orphanage called Saint Joseph's. Rumors about Saint Joseph's regarding all that took place there and the effect it usually had on those who went there reached my ears. Among other things, I heard about strictly enforced discipline and about younger kids being bullied. I was not encouraged, but with regard to other choices, I had none. All the other graduating students were applying to secondary schools. I was depressed because unlike them, I did not have options. It seemed that my life was already set in stone, without my having a say in my destiny.

The intensity of applying to secondary school is comparable to the experience high school seniors in the United States have when they apply to different colleges and universities. It was a big deal. In the midst of the excitement, I approached Sister Gabriel and told her that I had no wish to go to Saint Joseph's. She reminded me of my lack of options in the matter and asked me what I would rather do. I told her that I wanted to apply to Saint Ignatius College, a boarding school for boys. It was a prominent secondary school and consistently ranked as one of the best schools in the country, if not the best. She thought that I was a bit too ambitious given the circumstances. Nevertheless, in my heart I felt that I belonged there. I had fantasized about being there and imagined myself attending classes with fellow classmates. I had seen myself working on projects and playing sports in the fields. It was so close to reality, I was convinced that I could nearly touch it, but I lacked the resources.

Sister Gabriel told me that if it would help me sleep at night, I could apply. However, it would only be for the knowledge that at least I had tried. So I did. There was an entrance examination that all applicants had to take. I reported to the campus and sat the exam. It was a tough test, but I passed it. I would add that I did not pass with flying colors by any means. When you had passed that exam, you had to have an interview with the headmaster and his deputy. When my turn came, I was ushered into the headmaster's office by a Saint Ignatius prefect. The headmaster and his deputy were both there. The headmaster had a wonderfully unique accent that I could not exactly place. He asked me a question about my opinion on the state of the Zimbabwean political situation. I answered boldly to the best of my ability, and he chuckled at my remarks. He shook my hand and told me that I would hear from them. I returned home to play a waiting game.

One day Sister Gabriel came to me and told me that she had been thinking a lot about my situation, that she was impressed with my die-hard attitude, and that she wanted to make a call to the UNHCR about me. She requested my presence during the phone call. We went into the office of Mrs. Wasterfalls, the Emerald Hill social worker. Mrs. Wasterfalls placed a call to the UNHCR and explained my situation. The voice on the other end of the line said, "Refugees can go to any school they want. There are special funds for them."

I could not believe my ears. I looked at Sister Gabriel; she was so happy at the news that she stood there beaming at me. I would now benefit from a privilege because I was the thing that I dreaded to be called—a refugee. I concluded that sometimes it is not that bad to be labeled the thing that you are. I was ecstatic. I began behaving as if I had already been admitted to Saint Ignatius.

After some months of waiting, I finally received an envelope from Saint Ignatius College. I was aching to open it. That same day one of my good friends at school received his response from Saint Ignatius. His was a regrets letter. He was considerably smarter than I was and had obtained higher results on his entrance examination. My initial excitement became apprehension.

I tore open the envelope and offered a silent prayer. I looked at the letter. "Dear John, . . . we regret to inform . . ." I did not read on. I guessed what the rest would say. I sat down to calm myself. I felt as if I had been kicked in the stomach and left on the curb. I could not believe my eyes. I started thinking about how sure I had been that Saint Ignatius was where I belonged. Now I would have to go to Saint Joseph's. In my zeal, I had applied to only one school, with every confidence that I would be admitted. Old thoughts began sneaking into my head. "You should have seen it coming, refugee boy. You are not entitled to anything good." By the time I finished crying like a toddler, I had made up my mind that my new reality was exactly what I deserved for thinking that I was better than everyone else. Who was I, anyway? Shouldn't I go to Saint Joseph's like everyone else?

I put the regrets letter back in its envelope. I took it to Sister Gabriel, handed it to her and walked away without speaking. I was too embarrassed. She stood there watching with a confused expression on her face. My thoughts solidified to a conclusion that dreaming was for fools. You only got hurt.

The following days I kept to myself. I was not as loud as I usually was. I was lost in thought and could not shake the feeling that Saint Ignatius was for me. I would kneel in prayer, professing my fervent conviction that I still felt that Saint Ignatius was where I belonged, despite what the letter said. After praying, I sometimes felt better and encouraged myself by thinking, "They may have not admitted me, but they made a mistake, and they will reverse their decision." I felt a great impression that this would be the case. I was supposed to be making my preparations for Saint Joseph's but I did not. Furthermore, I did not dare reveal my conviction that the situation would be reversed because I was sure it would be met with ridicule.

A number of days went by, and Sister Gabriel came to me in the dining room and invited me to step outside with her for a minute. She handed me a letter that looked to be on Saint Ignatius College letterhead. I unfolded it to read: "Dear John, . . . after further review, we are pleased to inform you that you have been admitted . . ."

Sister Gabriel's eyes lit up as I embraced her with unrestrained exuberance. I was overwhelmed at the power that had turned my situation around. All I had done was exert my faith that the results I wanted would transpire, even when I did not have a tangible reason to believe that they would. This was cause for celebration. I ascribed this change in circumstance to God and to the faith I had exercised in Him. I found out later that Sister Gabriel knew the rector at Saint Ignatius and had successfully petitioned him on my behalf for admittance. When I learned this, I changed my mind and decided that maybe God had not played such a big part in it after all, now that I knew what had really happened. I have since learned that my attitude was a classic mistake. Countless times in history, men have seen unexplained wonders like lightning, thunder, and reversals of fortune and ascribed them to God. Then science or other sources have revealed the explanations behind these events, and these same men, knowing the explanation, revoke their belief in the hand of God in the matter. I now know that the explanation is God's method as well, His reward for putting our trust in Him before we understand the reason.

To this day, I am still grateful for Sister Gabriel's hand in the matter, and I believe that her faith in both the rector and me moved her to act for my benefit. She was the closest thing to a mother I had during my stay at Emerald Hill as an orphan.

◙

The following January I was to start school at Saint Ignatius. I was the first boy from Emerald Hill to go to a school like it and probably the first and only who did not go to Saint Joseph's. No one, especially my fellow orphans, had ever thought that was something that an orphan from Emerald Hill could do, mostly because it had never been done before. I have seen that many people are reluctant to take on a challenge simply because it has never been surmounted before. But everything that can be achieved by human beings had to be accomplished for the first time.

I was sad to leave my siblings for boarding school. This would be the longest that we would be separated, but we all knew it was a necessary change. When I left Emerald Hill, there was a bit of a parade. Most of my fellow orphans and the matrons were there to wave good-bye and wish me luck.

Sister Gabriel drove me to the outskirts of Harare, where I boarded a bus that took me to Saint Ignatius. I had a trunk that contained everything I would need for the school term. I had received a list from the school, which included the specific uniform, part of which included a gray shirt and shorts. This was to be worn Monday through Friday; therefore I needed multiple uniforms. They were expensive. Sister Gabriel had a friend, also a nun, named Sister Tarisai, whose nephew had attended Saint Ignatius for a few years. He still had his old school uniforms, so he donated them to me for my use. The only problem was they were as faded as gray could get, so faded that you could have mistaken it for a former white. When I reported to school the first day, I stood out in my faded uniform among the polished children of government ministers, businessmen, doctors, and lawyers.

Saint Ignatius was located in Chishawasha, a few miles out of the city of Harare. It also was perched at the top of a small hill just like Emerald Hill. Acres and acres of trees and other greenery surrounded it. It boasted three large fields that we used for rugby, soccer, and track. There were three basketball courts, a court for volleyball, and a large swimming pool for competitive swimming. The campus was intersected by mainly dirt roads that led from one set of buildings to the other. The dormitories were well separated from the classrooms and the administration building.

Our living quarters were separated into respective houses. Junior House was for forms 1 and 2, Middle House for forms 3 and 4, and Senior House for forms 5 and 6. Saint Ignatius was an all-boys academy until after form 4. In forms 5 and 6, girls were welcome to attend. They lived in Mary Ward, which was a separate building behind our classroom buildings. The other houses were on the opposite side of Mary Ward; therefore, the classroom buildings were between the girls' quarters and the boys'.

Because there were no girls our age, seeing the Mary Ward girls was an eventful occasion for us lowerclassmen. Whenever a group of girls from Mary Ward walked by our classrooms, we would flock to the windows to watch them walk away. When such an occasion presented itself in the presence of a teacher, however, we found a way to restrain ourselves.

Junior House was a single-story building that, from the air, was shaped like a capital E. It was adjacent to Middle House, which was a two-story building. Senior House was also a two-story building and stood a distance apart from the other buildings. In the chapel to the northeast of Junior House we attended mass on Sundays. Our choir practice was held there as well. The dining house was east of the chapel, and all three boys' houses convened there for meals.

Saint Ignatius was run on an institutional system of seniority. Everyone knew his or her place. The lowerclassmen could not enter the upperclassmen's classrooms or dormitories without incurring a serious beating. Freshmen at the school were stuck with the duty of waiting on the upperclassmen during meals. This, of course, was the best opportunity for them to humiliate us. I, a natural smart mouth, was an easy target for them. I didn't feel like I owed anyone respect just because they were older than I. I resented authority. The prefects had nearly as much authority as the teachers. We addressed them as "Elder." When they walked into our classroom, we were required to stand. I loathed this practice and filed a formal complaint to the headmaster. It went unheeded.

The level of education at Saint Ignatius was excellent, and we learned a great deal about the exact sciences and the social sciences. Sports activities were integral to the curriculum. I was on the junior basketball team and enjoyed our basketball games against other schools. Our games would require us to leave class early, and we relished the opportunity to skip the last boring stretch of class. When basketball season ended, I played on the junior rugby team.

We had a set schedule, much as I'd had at Emerald Hill. We woke up early, around six in the morning, and took our showers. We dressed in our uniforms and were inspected by the prefects, who looked in our lockers and checked our beds to see that they were well tended. Then we went to breakfast. Afterward we reported to our classes. We had short breaks between consecutive classes. Lunch was in the dining house. After lunch we could play sports or study. In the evening we had dinner, after which we would study until our respective bedtimes.

Though the Saint Ignatius law was not entirely rigid, I still managed to have a brush with it through Brother Kaputi, our religion teacher and head of Junior House. He oversaw the smooth running of Junior House. As a Catholic brother, he had taken a vow of celibacy. However, it had long been suspected that the woman who ran a small store at Saint Ignatius was his girlfriend. I do not recall where that suspicion began, but it was a common joke among us that Brother Kaputi entertained the young lady in his quarters late into the night. On one occasion, my friend Makoni and I went to use the public telephone but found this lady already engaged in conversation on it, monopolizing the time.

Makoni and I lost our tempers and started calling her names. She went straight to Brother Kaputi and told him an exaggerated version of what had taken place. I was called into Brother Kaputi's office after Makoni had been talked to. I was as nervous as it is possible to be. I feared that I had jeopardized my time at Saint Ignatius. Brother Kaputi confirmed this fear—the first thing he said was that we were to be expelled from school.

After interviewing Makoni and me separately, however, he decided our stories corroborated each other. He did the only thing he could do—he vented his anger on us, threatening to report us to our parents. He told us that if he saw us in his office ever again it would be the end of us. Luckily we were neither expelled nor reported to our parents. Brother Kaputi scared us enough that we comported ourselves well from then on.

I spent only a year at Saint Ignatius. It was my best year in Zimbabwe, and I made friends for a lifetime. Saint Ignatius was even better than I had imagined, and I went away proud to be an alumnus.

I did not return the following year because the adoption procedure was making headway. Three long years had elapsed since my aunt had started the battle to adopt my siblings and me. One last document was required before our file could be finalized. That document was my mother's death certificate, and I was the one to secure it.

I knew where I had to go. The offices of the ministry opened around 8:00 A.M. At 7:00 A.M. I was standing in line. You usually found long queues at these offices. They were always so crowded and so loud that the functionaries were always on edge. The doors opened, and we surged in. I found myself in a large reception area. A counter ran from one end of the room to the other. About eleven clerks stood behind the counter in what appeared to be booths. There were a few vacant chairs opposite the counter. At the end of the room was a corridor that led to another office.

I stood in line until my turn came. I walked up to the counter and requested the document I had come for, and the lady told me to sit down while she located it. I calculated that since I had come early enough, it would not take more than thirty minutes to retrieve the document. An hour went by, and I still had not heard from the woman who was helping me. I approached her to enquire about the reason for the delay. She told me to sit down and be patient.

Another hour went by and more people came in and many left. By noon, I still had not received the document, and the place was chaotic. The functionaries were yelling at the top of their lungs for names of people who had requested this or that document. By then, I was hungry and as irritated as I could be. When I approached the lady again, she beckoned to me to come to the back of the office.

"I want to show you something," she said. She let me in at the end of the counter, led me to a door, and opened it to usher me inside.

"This is where the document you want is located. And as you can see they are looking for it," she added, pointing to her colleagues inside. I poked my head in to look and was appalled. I saw mountains and mountains of files that were lying in a huge room that measured some thirty by sixty feet. Only three functionaries were there digging through the piles. I realized that I would be there for much longer than I had expected.

By six in the evening, my patience was completely worn out. I had been standing all day, in the heat of the day, with no air-conditioning to extend some comfort. My feet were aching from standing, and I was sweaty and irritated. I thought I was hungrier than I had ever been. I had not taken a break to eat lest my document be found when I was not present to claim it.

I suddenly found that I could not stay a minute longer or I would lose my mind. With my head hanging low, I walked out of the building, pushing my way through the crowd. I decided I needed some time to relax my nerves and chose to take the long way home. I wanted to punish myself by remaining miserable for as long as I could. Every step I took increased my irritation. Only one document stood between staying in Zimbabwe and going to Belgium, but I was walking away defeated.

Fortuitously I ran into my godfather, Egide. After a brief exchange he enquired after the reason for my presence in that part of town. I briefly explained what had happened. He looked at me sternly and with an imposing authority said, "You go back there and sit there until they give you that document. Don't you dare leave without it!"

I hurried back to the office, and the second I set foot inside I heard my name being yelled out. "Bizimana! Bizimana!" I walked toward the booth where the woman I had interacted with earlier was brandishing the document in the air. She seemed to be looking for my face in the crowd. Then she saw me, smiled an enormous smile of relief, and handed the document to me with much delight.

I offered my gratitude and walked out of the office with my chest swelling. I was ashamed of my earlier impatience and thought to myself, "What if?" What if I had not met Egide? Was it a chance meeting? What if I had been a minute later? A minute later would have been a minute too late.

To travel to Belgium we needed visas and passports. We had

neither. The Belgian government was going to issue us a travel document and a visa. In the previous three years my aunt and uncle had made a massive effort to raise the funds to purchase airfare as well as pay the lawyers. Many different fees had been demanded to locate all the documents that were required. My aunt and uncle had purchased airline tickets, but the Belgian embassy in Zimbabwe still had not delivered our travel visas. On the very day that we were scheduled to fly out, our visas were still not in our hands. Our tickets were nonrefundable. When we drove from Emerald Hill, we were not sure that we were going to be able to board the plane. Three years of labor had culminated to the point where the embassy had to deliver, or fail to.

To everyone's astonishment, we drove to the embassy and collected the visas and travel documents, which had arrived that very morning from Brussels. We went straight to the airport to catch our flight.

Despite the uncertainty of the circumstances, I was convinced that we were going to board that plane. We did not have our travel documents, and we did not have our visas. If we had decided that the situation was too uncertain for us to pack our bags and get in the car and instead had chosen to stay home and wait for the perfect conditions, we would not have gone to Belgium.

I was sad to leave Zimbabwe. It had been my home for the previous eight years. I had enjoyed the best years of my life there but had also mourned my worst. I knew that Zimbabwe would always hold a special place in my heart because my mother was buried there. I had made friends and even become part of a Zimbabwean family. The Denderes were there to see us off.

We hugged each other tightly, and they gave us a present to give to our aunt. We hugged Sister Gabriel, who had been our mother at the orphanage. She gave us some money for emergencies. Our hearts were heavy, but we were also excited about a new future—in particular, a future that would bring me closer to America.

Chapter 8

BELGIUM

We landed in Belgium the next day. We had flown from Harare to Heathrow, England, through Johannesburg, South Africa, and then from Heathrow to Brussels, Belgium. I was excited to be counted among the ranks of those who had flown in an airplane. I had to pinch myself to be sure I was truly awake in these tides of time through which my history was defining itself. Denial still weighed heavily on my zeal and restrained it from outwardly manifesting itself. Yet finally I was in Belgium, closer to America, and it was not just a distant dream or a figment of my vivid imagination.

My aunt Godelieve and uncle Felicien were at the airport waiting for us, along with their eldest daughter and another nephew of theirs who was filming our arrival. I recognized their faces, though showing the effects of age, from the photo albums my mother had returned home to retrieve eight years before, when we had taken up temporary residence at the stadium.

We saw them as we walked through the arrivals gate, and we met exuberantly, rejoicing in the embrace of many seasons lost in exile. We held each other and reveled in the joy of a reunion that had been postponed for far too many a year. Here was the woman who had raised my mother. Now she was to render to me the same maternal service. An overwhelming sense of triumph enveloped us in our prolonged hugs and kisses. Waves of familial affection swept over us. Pictures were taken to immortalize the moment that had taken three hard years to attain. Now we could gaze into the photographs and watch our arrival video to summon at will the warm sensations that we felt in this glorious moment. Victory was ours to claim. Its sweet savor far exceeded the sour mocking of the hindrances that had threatened to drown us in impossibility.

Oh, how capricious life is—to be told in one moment that this was simply not possible, and then in the next moment, that which was impossible became an emblem of defiance, imprinted on videotape and photo paper to put to naught the mighty words of the learned and their expert counsel. I was to be adopted, have a legal mother and father, and be an orphan no more. I would be among my own people, my real family.

We exited the arrivals area with euphoria still flooding us. We found our way to the parking lot, where we located my uncle's Volkswagen Golf. His nephew had also brought a vehicle. This new place was cold—indeed, very cold compared to the scorching African sun I was accustomed to. We loaded our bags into the trunks of the cars and drove from the airport on the outskirts of Brussels into the city.

Belgium was an odd-looking place; the buildings seemed

like a nineteenth-century movie set. It looked nothing like Zimbabwe. The roads were narrow, and some streets, I thought, looked as if they could fit only one car at a time in any direction. In downtown Brussels were skyscrapers like those I had seen in Harare, but there were fewer trees and green areas. The traffic looked different as well. A wider range of vehicles populated the roads; a few looked ridiculously beaten down and yet seemed to defy the ravages of time.

Most confusing to me was that the cars were being driven on the right-hand side of the road. In Zimbabwe they were driven on the left. *How do they shift gears with their right hand?* I thought to myself. As we passed through Brussels, I was mesmerized, fidgeting on the edge of my seat as I looked all around at the buildings we passed and measured up the different sights that my eyes beheld. *We are here! We are finally here,* I thought to myself. Emotion stretched my lips from cheek to cheek to smile at this wonderful day.

We parked in front of a massive church in the city center, a place called Sainte Catherine. I was surprised to see my uncle and the rest of the entourage carry our bags through the back door of this edifice and right into it. Were we going to live in a church?

My curiosity was promptly answered as we walked down a lighted hallway to find a door that led to a two-bedroom, one-bathroom apartment with a kitchen that took up part of the living room. It was to be our home. My uncle had taken on the daily duty to open and shut the massive doors that were the entrance to the church. In return he could occupy this apartment while paying minimal rent. My siblings and I were to sleep in

*John and his family in Belgium. From left to right: Uncle Felicien;
Angel, age twelve; Mary Yvette, age thirteen; John, age fifteen;
and Aunt Godelieve, in Brussels, Belgium, 2002.*

one bedroom, which had been my uncle's office before our arrival. It measured about five by ten feet and had a bunk bed. My brother took the top bunk, my sister the bottom, and I slept on the floor. A sense of our new reality crept up and settled on me. I felt ill knowing that our struggle with poverty had chased us halfway across the globe only to prolong its stay in our company.

In spite of my slight disappointment with the accommodations, the first few days were nevertheless breathtaking. My uncle acquainted us with our new surroundings, taking us to see Brussels. We went to see the royal palace and the royal gardens and other landmarks of European history. We rode on the subway, which was by far the most exciting thrill. We saw a monument named the Atomium in Laeken, a suburb of Brussels.

The Atomium is a giant structure in the shape of an iron atom, with restaurants inside and wonderful views of the area. The Atomium stood close to the Stade Roi Baudouin (King Baudouin Stadium), which hosts Belgium's national soccer team and other major athletic events. He took us to see the famous Manneken Pis, a statue of a little boy urinating. Belgium was a fascinating tourist attraction, and our first days there passed like a dream.

The first, and subsequently daily, reminder of our presence in Belgium was the communication barrier. My uncle and aunt attempted with relative success to communicate with us using the basic English they had learned during their sojourn in Kenya. Everyone else spoke French. That I was shocked to see white people who did not speak English would be an understatement. Until then, it was inconceivable to me that a white person would not speak English. As a natural consequence of the British colonization of Zimbabwe, almost every white person there spoke it. It had never crossed my mind that there existed other kinds of white people who spoke French, German, Spanish, and so forth.

That was not all. When I witnessed a white beggar on the street, I made up my mind that I had seen it all. You have to understand that all the white people I knew in Zimbabwe were wealthy, or at least financially stable. To see a white person who was neither was the shock of my life. Eventually our surreal fascination with our new country died down and made way for our gradual integration into our new life.

We started taking French classes so that we could one day be proficient enough to attend normal school. I understood absolutely nothing. I don't remember ever feeling more unintelligent and clumsy with locution. My French class was a melting pot of Portuguese, Spanish, Brazilian, and Zairean students and us. We went to class every day and learnt grammar and vocabulary. We had practice sessions in which we had to role-play. At home, my aunt and uncle spoke French to us, so as to exponentially accelerate our learning curve.

Some of the students in my classes were more advanced. I would attempt to repeat a phrase or sentence and in doing so make a classic mistake. Some of my classmates would giggle, even laughing out loud on occasion. I did not understand their thought process because their presence in class surely did not suggest proficiency. For eight hours a day, over a year's time, we attended French classes. Slowly but surely I learnt new words over the months. When people spoke, I did not understand most of what they said, but I would recognize a word or two and re-member what it meant from my French class. Over time, more words made sense, and I found myself engaging with more ease in French conversation.

After a few months, we moved out of the apartment in the church to another in Laeken, near both the Atomium and the stadium. My uncle worked for a housing complex in this area. He was able to procure an apartment easily because of his work. This apartment was larger than the previous one. It had three bedrooms: one for my aunt and uncle, one for Mary, and the last for Angel and me. Laeken was outside downtown Brussels and therefore quieter. This area was greener and had more facilities for sports. There were two outdoor basketball courts and a mini soccer field. It was a convenient location for public transporta-tion, and we had two general stores in the vicinity. By this time, I was sixteen years old.

As we eased into our new life, a double culture shock kept us from full immersion in this country's ways: one from the Rwandan community, and the other from the Belgian way of life. The Rwandans spoke Kinyarwanda, a language I did not speak. My aunt and uncle often participated in Rwandan activities, family visits, and so forth. Whenever we attended such activities, the other Rwandans asked us why we did not speak our own language. We were then compelled to tell the story that we had grown up in Zimbabwe after our mother died and that we were only exposed to English and Shona. These moments of explaining were awkward for me. I began to dread being among curious Rwandans. After numerous repetitions of such occasions, my siblings and I refused to attend any Rwandan events such as weddings and get-togethers. We did not like being spectators at their camaraderie and not participants. When asked where I was from, I would say Zimbabwe because in my heart I felt like a Shona. We spoke Shona among ourselves and even gossiped about people in their presence without them ever knowing.

The other shock came from the Belgian way of life, which was strange to me. It seemed that teenagers my age wielded more independence than I had thought possible for my peers. They publicly smoked and drank alcoholic beverages, which I believed to be strictly for grown-ups. There also seemed to be no sense of seniority. Lowerclassmen and upperclassmen interacted easily with each other. Children addressed adults by their first names. This was unheard of as well. I would not have dared to address an adult without a title of respect, such as *monsieur, madame,* or *mademoiselle.*

Two children of my aunt and uncle had been born in

Belgium and one in Canada. They were all considerably older than we were. Willy was in his late twenties, and Marie Louise— Malou for short—was in her early thirties. They both lived in Belgium. James, the youngest, lived in Canada. He was in his mid-twenties. Malou had two children, Arlette and Amaryllis. Both were very small, and her husband lived in the United States. At the time we arrived in Belgium, Malou was about to depart for America. I was jealous to the core that she would be leaving to live my dream. When she left, so did my heart, as I imagined her journey, the places she would see, the people she would talk with, and the life she would lead. I resolved that my turn would come soon and that my day lay close at hand. I did not know that I would not know such a day for another four particularly long and trying years.

◘

As required by law, when we arrived in Belgium we reported to the *commune,* the administrative headquarters. We went there a few days after our arrival armed with our travel documents and visas. The administration building stands in downtown Brussels and boasts about five floors. We went to the second floor, where we were required to appear. After standing in line and waiting our turn, my aunt presented our documents to the functionary. After a brief exchange, I could tell that my aunt was very upset. It was later explained that the visas we had been issued were the wrong ones. They permitted us to stay in Belgium for only three months, after which we were expected to leave the country. I thought it a prank by the Belgian government, and my aunt could not believe that after three long years of compliance with all the rigorous requirements, the Belgian government had still managed to default on its end by issuing us the wrong visas.

This nerve-wracking experience set us back by years; we were devastated. It would take another five years for me to get my Belgian citizenship, and four for Angel and Mary. The following years that I spent in and out of court battling for my legal rights instilled in me an intense hatred for bureaucracy. Unfortunately, western Europe is run by it. All the same, at the time that we received the first wave of bad news, I took comfort in the fact that my plan was not to be there for long. In my mind, I was heading to America very soon.

□

The transition from Zimbabwe to Belgium was uncomfortable. It came at the best of times but also at the worst; the best of times for us because shortly after we left, the economic situation in Zimbabwe spiraled down into an abyss that left almost everyone we knew destitute. Zimbabwe's economy soured to the point of having the highest inflation rate in the world, while infrastructure and whole industries collapsed. Our move also came at the worst of times because my teenage growing pains surfaced. I watched MTV and saw kids my age doing what they liked, some of them making or having more money than I could dream of. My immediate surroundings also reflected the same conditions.

My allowance was fifteen Euros a month, the equivalent of fifteen dollars at the time. With those fifteen Euros, I was to pay for my toiletries, clothes, shoes, and all other needs except food. That was all our aunt could afford to give us. There was only one place in Brussels where we could afford to go shopping with such a small allowance, and that was Clémenceau. It was an open marketplace with poor-quality goods of every kind. They had clothes, shoes, electronics, fruit, vegetables, and so forth. It also housed a butchery, to which many came from far and near to buy meat. A distinctive smell from the butchery welcomed you when you set foot near the market. Vendors were aggressive and yelled their prices at the top of their voices to drown out their competitors. They solicited every penny you had.

On Saturdays, one of us children had the task of going to buy fruit in Clémenceau. It was the cheapest place to get it. On those occasions you could also spend a Euro or two on socks and ten Euros on a new pair of shoes with a short life span. Then you would be left with about three Euros to pull you through the month. When you didn't have to make a major purchase, such as a pair of shoes or a new sweater, you could put aside five Euros for emergencies and use ten Euros to buy toothpaste, body lotion, and some Vaseline. If any was left, you saved it for emergencies, too.

In those times of not having much money, I felt worthless. In school, everyone recognized the brands of the clothes and shoes I wore as poor-quality Clémenceau merchandise. This made me feel inferior and hurt my self-esteem. I was also the oldest student in my classes because my siblings and I had spent a year taking intensive French classes so we could attend normal school. I had also repeated the second grade in Zimbabwe. Although I had studied French for a year, I still made mistakes when I spoke. I was afraid to participate in class because of the probability of making a grammatical or pronunciation error. I felt stupid for not being with classmates of my age. I was ashamed about my age and lied about it. I did not like school anymore in this setting, which never failed to remind me of my lowly rank in society. I started to seriously consider that school was perhaps not meant for me.

When I watched American television, I naturally identified myself with African-Americans. I had found a similar occurrence true for white Europeans in Zimbabwe. They naturally identified themselves with white Zimbabweans who had been born and raised there for many generations. They had nothing in common other than the color of their skin. Likewise I figured that if I were to be in America, African-Americans would be my reference. I saw that many had made names for themselves in the fields of singing, dancing, rapping, and sports. I decided that if anything, my calling in life had to correspond with one of these disciplines. Academic pursuits were not an option; I detested being at school.

I set out to find my vocation in life. I started with singing, but my voice sounded horrible. I would go every day to my sister, Mary, perform a demonstration of my singing skill, and ask her if my voice had improved from the previous day. To my dismay, she always provided a negative response. I concluded that singing was not the vocation for me. I tried rapping, but I could not connect rhyming words to save my life. Mary thought that I was a dreadful impersonation of an otherwise skilled rapper. Basketball was my favorite sport so I tackled that, but I never so much as neared stardom. When I failed in all these categories, I was crushed.

With my self-esteem shattered, legal battles continuing over our residency in Belgium, and my disappointment that I was still not in America, I seriously contemplated committing suicide. It seemed appealing to my newly discovered volatile personality. I asked my friends' opinions regarding the easiest and most painless way to end one's life. Most suggested an overdose of sleeping pills and jokingly asked if that was within my scope of consideration. *"Bien sûr que non—tu crois que je suis fou?"* was always my reply, which meant, "Of course not—you think I'm crazy?"

As is often the case with those who are most convincing of their innocence when most guilty, they believed me in that fraud of a reaction. My peers believed that considering such extreme measures was out of character for me; indeed, you would never have guessed otherwise. If you had judged by the countenance I showed to the world, you would have dismissed me as a hopeless attention seeker. But when left alone, I was squirming in my own skin. I do not remember why I never acted on the recurring impulse to take my own life, but I housed a lot of anger, and it yearned for an exit.

One of my best friends smoked marijuana. When he started smoking what the gangs sold, he developed an addiction to it. Very soon, in his hapless attempt to sustain his habit, he owed money to one of the gangs. So they told him to join them, hustling other kids to earn the money he owed—or else. He joined the gang out of fear of incurring the wrath of the gangbangers. You could not joke around with that lot.

My friend told me that if it was money I sought, there was a lot to be made in the gangs. They preyed on white, rich-looking Flemish kids and hustled them for electronics, cell phones, and cash. They also sold what they smoked in their respective areas of assumed authority. This was easy money. Black gang members capitalized on the white Flemish kids' fear of stereotypical black gangbangers' supposed tough demeanor, an afro or braids, tattoos, and sometimes facial scars from street fights. Because of the fear this appearance engendered, violence was not always necessary to procure submission for their demands. Black kids also fell victim to such bullying and were afraid of these gangbangers as well. I thought about the proposal my friend had made. I was seventeen at the time.

Before I could make a decision, my friend invited me to accompany him on a job so I could witness for myself how easy the money was. One night I found myself with him, in a poorly lit area named Simonis, which was dangerous after dark. We stood waiting while people and groups of kids made their way home. I don't remember ever being as nervous as I was that night. I knew I was betraying my conscience and stepping over a line from which retreat would be difficult. When my friend spotted a younger-looking, unaccompanied Flemish kid, he made his way toward him. My friend stopped the kid and demanded some money, but the Flemish kid was reluctant. Before I knew it, my friend had punched the kid right in the mouth, fished his wallet from his pocket, and fled the scene with me trailing behind him. I glanced back at the kid to see blood oozing from his mouth. My friend and I finally went our separate ways, but that night I did not sleep a wink. My conscience condemned me, and I knew to my core that I was not a violent person.

As I thought of that Flemish boy that night, my conscience was illuminated to the misfortunes we shared. He was hustled because of the life he had inherited. Most of the kids who fell victim to the gangs looked well-off, but it was not an offense toward anyone to be so; in fact, I desired to attain the same. In the past I had been discriminated against for my own past and the life that had been thrust upon me. In my own conscience I could not be the author of such discrimination. Once you were initiated into a gang, you could not quit, even if you felt inclined to. Your future was already set in stone the minute you pledged: you would end up either dead or in prison.

My friend was lucky not to come to a tragic end that would have otherwise been inevitable. His family moved to another part of the world. After serious reflection I decided I did not want to render my mother's efforts futile. She had saved me from the war and defended me all the way to Zimbabwe only to die herself. Was this, then, the way my life story would end? It was a sad end to submit to. Gang-related activities would not be the outlet of my anger; instead, I took up weight lifting, but I was still poor and miserable.

Naturally, I needed a scapegoat, someone to blame for my unhappiness. My foremost victims in this gloomy phase of my life became my aunt and uncle. I held them responsible for all that was amiss in my life. I charged them with snatching us from Zimbabwe when our lives were improving. As a natural consequence of absent parents in my youth, I had grown to considerable independence, a condition that proved to be in direct conflict with my aunt and uncle's respective maternal and paternal tendencies. In rebellion, I refuted their parental claims over me and challenged their jurisdiction over liberties I believed were due me. My raging hormones pushed me to the offensive and kept me on edge, forever seeking an altercation. My actions at this time alienated me from activities that could have facilitated bonding with them. My uncle is the most peaceful man I know, however, and he was able to remain aloof. Any grasp of civic duty and responsibility that I may now have, I owe to him.

Many questions went unanswered about the course that my life had taken. I felt that my life was cursed; I could not recall a time when I had associated happiness with my lot in life. I had not seen the reward in my efforts to be a good kid in a bad situation. I could not get what I wanted. I had always been a devout Christian and firmly believed in divine intervention. So I prayed and prayed for clearer skies and greener grass, but my skies remained cloudy and my grass parched. I concluded that believing in divine providence was useless. Such a belief promoted reliance on the said divine providence, which in turn curbed my personal effort, limiting it to feeble exertions that anticipated deliverance at any moment.

In the darkness of those teenaged years I lost my faith. I did not understand how a loving God could permit what had happened to me. Therefore I resolved that there was no God. I felt aligned with my mother, who in her wheelchair had forsaken Him. Joining with her, I scorned a nonexistent God with much satisfaction. I quickly forgot my dream of going to America. I accepted what others saw as the reality of my situation. Under the circumstances, I could not go to America. I had absolutely no leverage, no support, and no light at the end of the tunnel. All my hopes and desires were shattered by stark reality, a reality that left nothing to the imagination of a once-upon-a-time dreamer of a better life in a foreign land, a land of promise, a land of dreams that came true and drew their vitality from a deep well of endless opportunity.

◘

When I left Zimbabwe, I had dreamt that the grass would be greener and that I would not have any more problems. I had supposed that anything other than Africa was surely better. But people in Europe also had problems. Africans just had different problems. They battled for basic necessities, whereas the Europeans had these. Europeans, however, were plagued by social maladies, most of which I had never witnessed in Africa.

In retrospect I went to Belgium naïve and unprepared. I had unrealistic expectations formed in a misinformed mind. Many factors play into the dynamics of the events that influence our lives. One has to learn patience while one endures; time is the absolute refiner of character. So it goes in life that we intimately know many defeats but are acquainted with fewer victories. That is the way it is—some must be first while others are last. The distance between today and our dreams coming true tomorrow is patience. We must wait our turn. If that were not the case, we would all be trampling on each other's dreams.

Chapter 9

MISSIONARIES

In August of 2004, I was to turn eighteen. I had lived in anticipation of the day when the sun would go down on my last day as a juvenile. The reins of independence would finally be mine to guide my destiny wherever the trail of my imagination led. I relished the thought of never having to bow to anyone's dictates that were not in accordance with my will. I would be my own man and come home whenever I felt inclined to. I could sign my own report cards and deal with my own legal papers. School would not be compulsory anymore. If I woke up too weary to attend school, I could opt to stay at home instead. If my teachers were unsatisfied with my performance, they could not complain to my legal guardian because I would hold that position, and their complaints would fall on deaf ears. I would be accountable to no one but me. As soon as I turned eighteen, I would acquire a set of rights and freedoms to which I was currently a stranger. Oh, what bliss to finally be a man!

During the hot summers in Brussels, Promo Basket, a recreation agency, organized street basketball tournaments multiple times a week, each time in a different neighborhood. These tournaments began in the early afternoon and lasted until the evening. This system was practical for the youth in the community because it gave them something to do when school was out for two months. With nothing else to do, they would have been loitering in the neighborhoods restlessly. Promo Basket did the young people in the community a great service. Although it was highly competitive, street basketball had a unifying effect, bringing together many people from different neighborhoods and communities and fostering a fraternal environment.

I was a regular basketball player, so I signed up to participate. I enjoyed being present in this setting. The atmosphere was particularly vibrant. There always was loud, blazing hip-hop music being played, with a DJ from a Brussels radio station. He also presided over the games and offered outstanding commentary on them. The intensity of the loud music was the heart of the setting. It would orchestrate the tempo of the games. The faster the beat of a song, the more animated and electrifying the game became. The energy was contagious and quite an attraction. Young people came in multitudes, and everyone knew each other, some intimately and others only by face. The street basketball tournaments were the epitome of the urban black neighborhood scene.

On one occasion, I decided to attend with one of my very good friends. I had spent the night at his home and therefore did not have my basketball gear. Consequently I would be limited to being only a spectator. When we reached the venue, the games had already commenced, and the atmosphere was highly charged. The basketball courts had been divided into smaller sections so that multiple games could be held at a time. Crowds were gathered around the courts cheering, jeering, jumping up and down, and rewarding every successful shot with an uproar. Most of the people present were dressed in street basketball attire. Headbands and bandanas were the norm, along with extra large T-shirts and baggy silk shorts that descended way below the knees, as well as Air Jordan, Nike, and other basketball shoes. Some participants were dancing and clapping to the loud music, and many were off to the side practicing their moves and tricks.

As we walked around nodding at acquaintances and acknowledging each other's presence, I noticed, in the corner of my eye, something that caused me to do a double take in surprise. There were two young white men in suits, white shirts, and ties. One of them was playing in one of the games. He was about 6'5" and would have stood out even in regular basketball gear. *How incongruent!* I thought to myself. These boys were really out of place. I was curious to know what on earth they thought they were doing there. I watched the one who was playing a one-on-one game while his colleague watched on the sidelines. I was amazed at how comfortable he seemed on the court in that attire. To my surprise, he won the game. He then walked back to his colleague to chat.

I approached them both and addressed the tall one in French, beginning the conversation with complimentary remarks. After a brief exchange, I concluded they were not from Belgium because of their heavy accents. I asked them where they were from, and they told me that they were missionaries from

America. When I heard that, my heart leaped. I did not know anyone from America. I started bombarding them with questions about their country and listened to their responses with thrilled anticipation. At one point during the conversation, the tall missionary, Elder Kruse, asked me politely to what I owed my presence in Belgium. I told him that I had come there to be adopted by my aunt and uncle. I was usually evasive when asked that question, but for some reason, I felt that I just had to tell him the truth.

"Why? What happened to your parents?" he asked.

"They died when I was younger," I replied, to which he said nothing. I was surprised by his casual reaction. People usually became awkward and apologetic when I told them my story. So I added, "You know, when most people hear that, they get awkward and apologetic, but you surprised me. You reacted differently."

With the same casualness he replied, "Oh, well, that's because I know where they are," and he confidently lifted his forefinger to point to the sky. All of a sudden the loud music and the cheering of the crowds were drowned out for a moment. I heard my heart pound in my ears. Space and time stopped and contracted into this spark of a moment. An overpowering feeling of peace overcame my being and gently enfolded my core as my mind processed what he had just said. Somehow, both that statement and gesture touched a nerve. It was as if I had always known the truth of it but had merely forgotten and was now being reminded. Although I had been told that my mother was damned for what she had said, I had secretly hoped that she would be saved. All of this was contradictory to my beliefs; I had decided that there was no God to save my mother. Despite it all, I found myself believing this missionary.

Of those emotions that overpowered me, I have only managed a feeble account with the limitations that language imposes. It would be little use to attempt a further description on a grander scale. Later on Elder Kruse and his companion, Elder Prusso, asked me if I would be interested in discussing some more, and I accepted their invitation. I wanted to hear what they had to say. A few days later, we held our first meeting at their chapel. They greeted me warmly when they saw me, and we found a room where the three of us sat down. The missionaries proposed that we start by singing a hymn. I did not know the hymn, so I listened to them sing. They were not the most able singers, yet they had the humility to go ahead and sing anyway. Then they told me the story of a boy in America named Joseph Smith in the nineteenth century, who had questions regarding the religious direction he should take in his life. The missionaries told me how the boy witnessed a vision in which he saw the Father and the Son. They related how this boy had later been guided to a place where he found ancient golden plates with writings on them and how, with the assistance of God, he translated these plates into a book that these missionaries had with them. As I listened to the story, I kept asking myself how on earth I had never heard of such a story before. At the end of the discussion, they handed me a copy of the Book of Mormon in English. They told me that it was similar to the Bible but that it pertained to the ancient inhabitants of the Americas and their dealings with God. These ancient people had compiled their history for hundreds of years, and this history was the Book of

Mormon. They invited me to read the book and pray about its message and find out for myself whether it was indeed a true account of the word of God or not.

I took the book that day and was anxious to start reading it, mostly because I had never heard of another book containing the word of God except the Bible. When I got home, I opened it to the first chapter of First Nephi and started reading. I first noticed the vivid similarity of the language to the Bible. I started browsing through the whole book and randomly stopped to read a passage, which happened to be the thirty-first chapter of the book of Alma, verse five. It read: "And now, as the preaching of the word had a great tendency to lead the people to do that which was just—yea, it had had more powerful effect upon the minds of the people than the sword, or anything else, which had happened unto them—therefore Alma thought it was expedient that they should try the virtue of the word of God." Joseph Smith wrote that when he read a particular scripture in the Bible in the book of James, that no scripture ever came to the heart of man more powerfully than that one did to his (see Joseph Smith–History 1:12). Likewise I would say that no scripture ever came more powerfully to the heart of man than that one from Alma did to mine. It became my favorite scripture because it made me think of the life I had led, the war, my parents, our poverty, and how none of that would ever have a more powerful effect upon me than the virtue of the word of God.

My mind, however, was in turmoil. I had decided I did not believe in God, but the discussions with the missionaries gave me peace and soothed my soul in a way that was familiar. I had felt this peace many times as a child when life was simpler and when my faith in God was abundant. Yet as I grew older and had more problems, I became more skeptical and finally lost my faith. I was led to reflect on the issue of losing one's faith. I concluded that I had not ceased believing in God; I only believed I had ceased. I was angry with Him for not being immediate in a way that was convenient for my ends. The discussions with the missionaries led to an invitation to be baptized in their church. I was unsure because I had been baptized as a baby. I told them I would think about it. Nevertheless, they encouraged me to attend their church, The Church of Jesus Christ of Latter-day Saints.

◘

On the first Sunday I was to go to church, I sat on a tram with my scriptures on my lap. I was nervous about getting to church on time because I did not know the way there. I had been given directions, but they had proved quite unclear to me. I planned to ask for more directions when I stepped off the tram. When the tram arrived at my stop, a tall African woman flanked by her two young children walked past me, stopped dead in her tracks, looked down at me in my seat, and with a smile on her face asked, "Are you coming to church?"

Her name was Regina Mukondola. She was a woman of graceful appearance and elegant proportions. I have seen but few African women of that class. As I walked with her to church, we held quite a pleasant conversation in which I learned that she was from Zambia and had lived in Belgium for the previous ten years. She had come to Belgium as a diplomat's wife with her four children, Claudia, Christopher, Louisa, and Mutale, whom they called Tale.

The church building was situated in a nice neighborhood called Strombeek. When I walked into the building, a few people came to meet me and introduced themselves. *What a cheerful lot these people are,* I thought to myself. I found myself feeling very comfortable among them.

As the meetings of that day progressed, I was impressed by the congregation. The people were so warm and so nice. They all seemed to get along with each other and were very affectionate and very expressive of their affection. As I sat in the congregation with Regina and her family, I saw husbands holding hands with their wives or gently rubbing their backs. They seemed to be happy to be in attendance. I was also struck by the presence of young people my age. In my past experience, I saw mostly old people in church. This place had a very peaceful tone to it, and I felt quite at home.

A few days after my first church attendance, instead of meeting with the missionaries at the chapel, they asked me if they could come over to my home for our discussion. I accepted. On the appointed day, there was a knock on the door, and I let them in. My aunt was present, and as soon as she found out who they were, I found myself at loggerheads with both her and my uncle. They both told me that this church was a cult and that I had to question the missionaries' intentions. They professed that they had heard a lot of unflattering things about this church and that they did not want me associating with it.

I was confused. The feelings I had felt the previous Sunday seemed genuine enough to me and I was confused at how a church with such nice people could correspond to the image my aunt and uncle had of it. They told my older cousin Willy, whom I respected considerably, and he tried to dissuade me from associating with the missionaries. I felt greatly discouraged and did not know what to do, but I reasoned that my aunt, uncle, and cousin were much older than I was; they had more experience and therefore knew better than I did. So I began to consider ending my relationship with the missionaries.

This prospect, however, made me uneasy when I reflected upon the good people I had met. Members of that church had been nice to me on that Sunday and had shown a genuine interest in me. There was also the lady from Zambia, Regina, for whom I already felt great respect. So I decided that I would lend these missionaries only my ear and not be baptized, but it was not long before they also won my heart. I felt in my heart that I needed to be baptized, and so I decided to go ahead with it, but I did not dare tell my aunt or uncle. This was something I had to do in secret or they would make me doubt myself again.

I remember that day distinctly—August 22, 2004—because there were quite a few people in attendance. A man by the name of Philip Lambert baptized me. Because it was his first time to baptize a person, he was just as nervous as I was, perhaps even more so. All went well, and he immersed me under the water in the baptismal font. As soon as I came back out, I saw everyone looking down at me. I did not know what to say so I raised my hand in a clenched fist and yelled "Yeah!" much to everyone's amusement.

A little reception was held in my honor to welcome me into the Church, and Regina was assigned to make some remarks

John at church with Regina Mukondola and his brother, Angel.

about baptism and the Holy Ghost. A young man who was about my age, by the name of Christian, addressed the topic of baptism in a thick African accent.

Of all the young men my age I knew, Christian was perhaps the most remarkable. He was a new convert to the Church as well, and his story was incredible. It included being born into the life of a hunter in the jungles of Ghana, living in poverty without electricity or running water, surviving a perilous voyage to Europe with his mother, being forsaken by her once they arrived in foreign territory, and finally attending school for the first time in his life when he was fifteen years old. The missionaries found him on the streets of Brussels and took an interest in him, even though they could not communicate with him. Other missionaries started teaching him his ABCs, and he gradually acquired reading and writing skills, although still on an extremely basic level. He was lacking in multiple areas, yet he was as confident as a person can possibly be. During our gospel discussions, he and I would take turns reading scriptures. When it was his turn, he would stutter and stumble over words, mispronouncing them, not understanding them, yet he kept on going in confidence. It was an amazing sight to behold. With unbelievable perseverance and hard work, Christian has since earned his GED and is now a college student.

After Christian's remarks at my baptism, the bishop officially welcomed me to the Church. He invited me to go home and write down all the feelings I had experienced on this fateful day that marked the beginning of a new life and the end of an old one.

The path to being an active Christian is never smooth. I faced considerable internal and external pressures that pushed me to recant the faith I had found. Perhaps the hardest challenge among all else was to unlearn old habits and learn new ones. To become the person I wished to be, I had to be drained of that of which I was full and to be filled with that of which I was barren. I had to forsake old attitudes and adopt new ones, end friend-ships that would lead me into trouble, give up my basketball games on Sunday morning to go to church, and so forth.

◘

Regina's terrific life story is worth a novel. She was the incar-nation of all that was independence, strength, and courage in a woman of character. For years, she had enjoyed the comfortable life of a diplomat's wife, until she separated from her abusive husband. In a story quite similar to my mother's, in an instant she lost all the privileges she was accustomed to but was still required to feed four other mouths while being unemployed and facing legal issues pertaining to her residency in Belgium. When she lost her diplomatic status, she became an illegal alien in Belgium and was required to leave the country. She calculated, however, that her prospects in her home country of Zambia would not be favorable to her and her children. She decided to stay in Belgium and, just as my mother had fended for us in our years of destitution, care for her children and put them through school. It is quite remarkable to observe today the caliber of the children she raised.

From the day I met her, I knew there was something special about her. She demonstrated, as if by instinct, maternal affection towards me even before she thoroughly knew me. I quickly became the best of friends with her children Chris and Claudia. We were about the same age. Chris exhibited ambition and intelligence, which to a dreamer like me was of great worth. I was also drawn to his charisma, and when he spoke English, he spoke it properly, foregoing the slang and Ebonics prevalent among those of my acquaintance. At first I labeled him a snob for not sounding like the black man that he was, which in itself was a misconception on my part. At length I grew to appreciate his originality. His faithfulness to his individual self gave me permission to become independent of the expectations I felt I had to meet as a black man in a white man's country.

Another reason Chris became my closest friend was his sense of humor. I recall a time I went to a dinner party with him, his mum, Regina, and the rest of his siblings. We had a wonderful time, and when the music started playing I asked his mum to dance with me. A few minutes into the dance, Chris, a cheeky look on his face, came to his mum and me and said, "May I have this dance?"

I immediately replied, "Of course!" and as I relinquished his mum to him, he came straight at me and attempted to dance with me instead. By this time I was bent over in laughter, and his mum was very amused as well.

Regina's younger children, Louisa and Tale, were bright young kids whom I embraced as siblings. My love for them increased until it almost rivaled the love I felt for my very own Angel and Mary. Over time, Regina's maternal nature blossomed to familial dimensions. Soon I was spending more hours at her home than mine. Time flew by as we enjoyed each other's company, mostly reminiscing about the good old days in our motherland, Africa. To her, I was the African son she had never had. To me, she was the African mother I had never had. All her children were very young when they left Africa and could not draw much from their memory of it; in fact, Tale was born in Belgium.

I, on the other hand, had spent fifteen years of my life on the motherland and for that reason among many she felt connected to me. Very soon I was addressing her as "Mother." She was the first African woman to tell me, "I love you." Even my own mother, whose womb had nurtured me for nine months, had never uttered those words to me. In the culture where I was raised, parents did not verbally express affection for their children. They professed it in their actions, which implied love in full. My mother had always cared for me, but she had never expressed her love for me in words. The Denderes in Zimbabwe came to love us but never verbally announced it. My aunt and uncle loved me as well, but they never expressed it out loud. In fact, one year on Mother's Day, my sister, Mary, decided to give our aunt a Mother's Day card. So Mary wrote in it how she appreciated all that our aunt did for us, taking care of us, cooking, cleaning, and so forth. When my aunt opened the card to read it, I could see that she was delighted. However, being emotionally reserved, she simply said, "*Je vois que vous avez améliorés votre grammaire en Français,*" meaning, "I see that you have improved your French grammar." That was all she had to say concerning Mary's gesture.

The first time that Regina told me she loved me, I was caught off guard and was not sure what kind of response would be adequately respectful. It was new to me. She opened my eyes to a new way of looking at life and taught me the absurdity of basing judgment about people along racial and cultural lines, to which I was partial.

I felt comfortable in this new church and around these new people. This occurred at a time when I was in desperate need of guidance and encouragement. I had barely turned eighteen and felt that I was finally fit to take my place among the ranks of men; however, I was far from being a man in those days. Being a man means more than being independent and much more than indulging in unrestrained, short-lived thrills that find sanction in the absence of accountability.

Perhaps one of the most important lessons I learned was to make decisions consistent with my conscience and not to make excuses for them. For instance, the decision I made to be baptized was aligned with my conscience, yet I did not dare tell my aunt. I could have told my aunt that my heart's desire lay in being baptized, but I lacked the courage. One day the missionaries called my home to invite me to another person's baptism, and my aunt answered the phone. Because I was not present, the missionaries invited her to attend, to which she responded that the only baptism she would ever attend would be mine.

"*Mais John est déjà baptisé*" they told her, meaning, "But John is already baptized." It is sufficient to say that it was truly an embarrassing occasion I endured when she informed me of this conversation. I was surprised to know that she would have laid aside her prejudices against this church for a day had I decided to approach her like a man.

With my energy newly rekindled from meeting all of these wonderful and ambitious people, I found my feet treading that road of dreaming again. My six-year-old dream of going to America had been reduced to dust and blown away in the winds of my experiences. When I had undergone hardships that challenged my hopes and desires, I shrank in defeat, fearing an unfavorable outcome. Now I remembered that I did not have to surely possess the means which could make my dream come true. I did not even have to wait for the ideal conditions, for there were none. I knew that I would have to seize my dream among the earthquakes and hurricanes that are life. My mind raced back to the time that I had dreamt of attending Saint Ignatius College but had no means. Because my way had been opened on that occasion, I was sure that my Saint Ignatius experience could be a model for all present and future aspirations. With those thoughts, my hope was revived.

◨

Getting to America would be a complicated process with its fair share of woes. I examined my options and found that I had two. The first was to enter the green card lottery, as my aunt Christine had previously done in Zimbabwe. This option appeared painless and would be of no cost to me. All I had to do was fill out the application form and wait patiently. It was easy. I did not have to exert myself. I did not have to think, and I did not have to toil. I was, however, repelled by the lack of control of one's destiny in that option. The chances of winning were dismally minimal.

The second option was to go to America as a student. This way seemed closer to a realistic expectation. But when I looked into the details and mechanics pertaining to this option, I realized that it was equally unrealistic as the first one, at least for me. It included effort, sweat, and toil. With foresight, I went through the usual checklist. Was this an overly ambitious project? Check. Were resources lacking? Check. Were there other reasonable options that an average person could live with? Double check. This, in my mind, meant only one thing: it was a challenge worthy of my time, and not only that, it was also definitely going to work. I just did not know how.

I started investigating schools that I could apply to, but there were so many. The United States is a huge country. Then someone at church suggested that I consider a school in Utah named Brigham Young University. I conducted my research and judged that it was a good university and it was cheaper than most good schools in the United States. No matter how cheap it might have been, however, I still could not afford to attend such a school.

Because I had benefited from my refugee status with respect

to school tuition at Saint Ignatius, I thought that it might not be a stretch of the imagination to assume the availability of the same kind of benefits in Belgium. I hunted down several humanitarian organizations in Belgium, went to them one by one, and requested financial aid. I explained my case in a heartfelt manner and told them that I was in desperate need. My auditors were usually sympathetic but could not offer help of any consequence to me. The same argument kept sneaking its way into the conversations: I could easily attend a Belgian school. Belgium boasted good schools that were within my price range, because I could request financial aid from the Belgian government to study there. The only problem with that option was that it was far from my dream and thus availed me nothing. I tried everything I could, but nothing was successful. I felt discouraged and defeated again because I had much to contend with.

At church I attended a youth group called Young Men. My Young Men's leader, Joseph Gordhamer from Minnesota, suggested that I take the SAT (Scholastic Aptitude Test) in the meantime, while I figured out the finances. He said it would help my application to do well on a test I was not required to take. As an international applicant, I was required to take the TOEFL (Test of English as a Foreign Language). I did not have to take the SAT. I did not see how it would help my application if my most significant need—financing—could not be met. The other significant issue was the intimidation I felt in thinking about that test, which contended with my reasoning. I had not taken a proper English class in four years. I had left Zimbabwe with a seventh- or eighth-grade English proficiency level. I feared that my English had become quite rusty. How could I then venture to take the SAT?

I researched where and when the tests would be held and found that they were to be administered at the international schools in a matter of less than three weeks. This was in June, already the most stressful month of the academic year. All large projects of the semester were due then; in addition, final examinations were held in this same month. I didn't feel I had the organizational skills to simultaneously balance studying for the SAT, completing my projects, and studying for final exams at my regular school. Feelings of inadequacy overwhelmed me. This seemed like an endeavor I could not successfully undertake in the time frame I was facing. With my qualifications, I was not going to do well on the SAT, which would frustrate the point of my taking it in the first place. However unsure I felt about it, I nevertheless had a deep impression in my heart that I needed to take it and prove myself, regardless of my supposed incompetence.

Regina's son Chris, who was also applying to universities across the United States, including Utah, had a copy of the SAT preparation manual that he graciously put at my disposal. By then, I had less than two weeks left before the test and less than a week to start my finals. I decided that in the short time I had, I would choose an area to focus on, either English or math. Shooting for both would result in my attaining neither. I decided to focus on English and neglect math, because the TOEFL was required to demonstrate proficiency in English. During the following two weeks, I did not sleep much. My normal school projects kept me awake until about 3:00 in the morning. I would then study for the SAT until around 5:30. I would then indulge in a thirty-minute nap and be up again by 6:00 to get ready for another school day.

Before I knew it, test-taking day was upon me. I did not have enough money for the test, so Joseph, my Young Men's leader, gave me fifty Euros to take the test. He had said that if I did not do well, I would owe him the money. I took two metros and a bus to get to the International School of Brussels (ISB), the school where the test was to be administered. ISB was located at the opposite end of Brussels from where I lived. I reported to the school that Saturday morning sleep-deprived and very nervous. There were about a hundred other students, most of them from ISB. We were ushered into our respective test-taking rooms.

When I had decided to take the test, I had already missed the deadline for registering online, so first I had to fill out a registration form in another room. I sat next to a white American girl. Her father was there leaning over her to help her fill out the form. I stole a quick glance around the room and saw several students with parents helping them fill out the form and supporting them through the test-taking process. In that moment, I felt quite alone. No one but Joseph, Regina, and I believed in what I was doing. No one else supported me, and no one who believed in me or cared about what I was doing was in this room with me.

I shrugged my shoulders and started filling out my form. When I got to the payment section, I was horror-struck. I had two problems. The first arose from my registering on the same day that I was taking the test. There was an additional late-registration fee, which made the total more money than I had brought. The second was that I could pay only by credit card. I had never had a credit card before. I could not believe my eyes, so I leaned over to the American girl to make sure.

"Hey, is it true that we can only pay by credit card?" I asked.

Her father leaned over to me and said, "Yeah, you need a credit card, man."

I leaned back into my seat and let out a sigh of defeat. The previous two weeks had been nerve-wracking. I had worked harder than I ever had before. I had allocated all my resources of time and energy into preparing for this day. I had really tried with all my might. I was slowly realizing that it had all been a big waste. As I was about to stand and find my way out, the man turned to me and asked me, "How much money do you have on you, son?"

I replied that I had fifty Euros. That amount failed to meet the full price by forty Euros.

In a miraculous moment of compassion, he said, "You know what, you can use my credit card. I'll take the fifty and we'll call it even. How about that?"

To this day, I am amazed at what happened. How could a man who did not even know me just decide to lend a helping hand while incurring a loss himself? Between this act of compassion and the demands of the test, by the time I walked out of the testing center my head was spinning.

◘

A few weeks passed. I had survived my finals at school, and I was waiting for my SAT scores. Every day I checked my mailbox in anticipation. I was hoping that I had done well. As I had walked out of the testing room I felt very discouraged. Chris had recently received his scores and had not done very well. This troubled me because his level of English was very advanced. I started doubting myself.

As on other occasions, my comparing myself to other people wrought unnecessary pain. When I compared myself to others, I walked away with a crushing sense of inadequacy as to my qualifications. I now know, however, that having some self-esteem independent of other people's abilities is integral to our well-being. We are all different and bound to have different capacities. To one is given a hammer and to another a saw. You cannot compare hammers and saws or you will end up upset that your hammer does not cut or your saw does not pound. My eyes were blind to this understanding when I most needed it.

One day the envelope that contained my scores finally arrived. I opened it apprehensively and inspected it to see what they were. I had scored a 570 on the math—no surprises there—and a 650 on the English, which totaled 1220 out of 1600. This score was good enough for me to forego taking the easier test (the TOEFL) that I was required to take as an international student. Under the circumstances I felt like this was once again another victory but by no means a knockout blow.

I was pleased indeed, for I had worked rigorously, but I did not know what to do next. Shortly thereafter Joseph, my Young Men's leader, returned to the United States. He had been my encourager, so his departure left me devoid of inspiration. Between his being gone and my growing dislike of waking up early to go to church, I slowly settled into inactivity. Although I had a spark in the beginning and enjoyed being at church, I preferred staying home on Sundays to relax. Church attendance came with responsibilities and a commitment to participate that I was starting to dislike. The other young men called me regularly to invite me back, but I would not budge. The commitment the Church required was now more than I was willing to pledge. So I alienated myself, being content to watch the American evangelist Joel Osteen on television on Sundays. A few weeks passed in this manner. I cannot recall how happy or unhappy with myself I felt, but one event changed it all.

One day in the mail I received an envelope. I hastily opened it and found a card inside. It had a drawing of the planet earth. Standing at both the top and bottom of the globe were two stick men. On the cover was written, "It feels like we are a world apart." I opened it and started reading. The letter inside said that I had been missed and that church was not the same without me. It added that we were all on a personal journey and that we did not need to be perfect to come to church. It continued along those warm lines and concluded by asserting that I would be in the sender's prayers. It was signed Kelly Kimball.

Kelly was a nice white lady from Colorado. I had met her at church and from day one she had been awfully nice to me. She always enquired after my well-being. Once, on my birthday, she gave me a birthday card with some money. I was fond of her, and her card touched me. Her kind outreach to me softened my heart, and I started contemplating returning to church. Sunday came, and I received a call from one of the young men by the name of Peter Hamilton. He asked me if I was coming to church that day, and I told him that I was unsure. He replied, "Get ready. We're coming to get you," and hung up. In a few

John at church with Kelly and Spencer Kimball.

minutes he was at my home with a number of the other young men and Kelly's husband, Spencer Kimball, the grandson of a previous Church president. So I got dressed and went to church with them, and from then on I never thought of quitting again.

One Sunday Spencer Kimball approached me and enquired after my college plans. I told him about my dream to go to America and to Brigham Young University but explained that I didn't have the resources and was therefore unsure how my dream would work itself out. He listened intently, and after that we spoke of something else. It must have been the next Sunday that he approached me again. "Let's talk," he said, and we stood apart to hold a private conversation. "If finances are the only thing stopping you, Kelly and I are willing to participate," he said. I thought I had not heard him right. The Kimballs did not know me that well. I could have been a drug dealer or a punk for all they knew; nevertheless, he told me that my dream now had the means by which to become true.

Over the years, I have had the privilege of getting better acquainted with the Kimballs. Both Kelly and Spencer took a special interest in me, and I do not know why. The more I got to know them, the more I grew in admiration for them. They treated me like one of their own, and as time has gone by, I now see them as my American parents. I have my aunt and uncle, who are my African parents; I have Regina, who is my Zambian mother. Ever since these people came into my life, I have reflected on the irony of my story. God took my mother away, only to bless me with multiple mothers. He took my father away, only to bless me with multiple fathers. In the end, I suppose that perspective is everything. Were it not so, I would still be lamenting lost parents instead of celebrating the ones I have won.

When I consider the histories and backgrounds of all the people I have interacted with, I cannot help but be impressed by the transcendence of compassion and love over cultural and racial lines. All the way from Rwanda, people with whom I was at odds in cultural, economic, and social status came to my relief. Many times they were from a different race, though in their own countries race was sometimes a matter of contention. In Zaire, local people had housed my family and me when we had no shelter. In Tanzania, the natives had fed us when we had no food. In Zimbabwe, a Shona family had loved us as though we were not from abroad. A German nun had cared for us when we had no parents. In Belgium, both Belgians and Americans had opened their hearts to me and welcomed me into their families as a long-lost son. In fact, another American family from Idaho, the Hills, told me that if I ever needed anything or a place to stay in America, I could always call on them.

Many of my experiences to this point had taught me to label differences in people, creating prejudice in my mind. Moreover, all the white people I had known in Zimbabwe had been well-off. Therefore, in my mind being white meant having more opportunities than black people. In Europe, however, I had seen poor white people who had less opportunity than some well-off black folk. It occurred to me then that opportunity did not knock exclusively on the door of white people but on the door of any who had the courage to build one.

My prejudice crumbled at the tenderness of the human hearts that had shown me kindness notwithstanding our differences. Ignorance had constrained me from looking at life and people objectively. Having different experiences with different people liberated me from a prison of preconceived notions. There was no reason why I and people of other races or simply of other cultures could not live together in harmony. I believe that all of us are in pursuit of some happiness, and if we cannot be of help to our fellowman, then let us at least not be a hindrance to them.

◇◆◇

Chapter 10

ACHIEVING THE DREAM

After I had spent almost four years in Belgium, the state of my citizenship was still unresolved. I did not have a valid travel document. The one the Belgian government had issued had been valid for the singular trip from Zimbabwe to Belgium. At the near-inert rate that our citizenship and adoption procedures were moving, I was certain that without an alternative, I would not see America within a reasonable time frame. Yet I finalized my application to Brigham Young University and felt somehow that I was a step closer to my dream. Unbeknownst to me, a great trial of patience awaited me.

I started deliberating on alternative ways to acquire a travel document. Out of the blue it occurred to me that I should apply for a Rwandan passport at the Rwandan embassy in Brussels. This was a brilliant idea. I wondered why I had not thought of such an obvious option earlier, but the explanation was simple. I had grown up avoiding any association with Rwanda for reasons already made clear. I still identified myself as Zimbabwean at heart, though from a legal standpoint it was a nationality I could not claim. Now my path to America entailed accepting what I truly was—a Rwandan. Speaking retrospectively, I am still not partial to the principle behind it, which was accepting my identity as defined by law. I was more sympathetic to the practicality of the solution.

I had been to the Rwandan embassy before, to request a birth certificate for the Belgian authorities. This time I went to the Rwandan embassy armed with the birth certificate they had issued, some passport-size photos, and the money they charged for the passport application fee, money that had been difficult to acquire. I exhausted my savings but the money was still insufficient by more than half the fee. My sister, Mary, drained her financial reserves to invest in my dream, much to her own fiscal detriment. She never doubted the surety of my dream coming true. In all my endeavors she had been my most trusted confidante. She fully recognized all that I lacked in character and wisdom; still, her faith in me was unfailing. Even when I was discouraged and stopped believing, she carried the torch in my stead until my motivation and inspiration had adequately recuperated for me to continue my struggle. I found myself pursuing a dream with my younger sister's carefully collected savings that would take me thousands of miles beyond her tender love.

I reported to the embassy, completed my application, and submitted it for processing. I was told that if all went well, I would receive my passport in a month, but should complications arise, it could take up to three months at the most. The embassy would contact me when my passport arrived from Kigali, Rwanda.

I went home that day radiating joy. The only remaining milestone to my dream coming true was admission to BYU. I had not bothered to apply to a Belgian school for the following academic year, owing to the confidence I had. I believed that with the stakes thus intentionally raised high, no other choice was worth considering but a victorious one. I had announced my assumed imminent departure to all my friends and acquaintances— failure to leave would have left me in a highly embarrassing position. In the following weeks, my nerves fluctuated from the highest highs to the lowest lows. I could not master my nerves.

After what seemed an eternity I finally received news from BYU. "Dear John, . . . we are delighted to inform you . . ." I did not read further for I knew what the rest would say. I was at the top of the world, desperately trying to absorb the wonderful tidings with some restraint, but such an attempt was futile.

At that point, I would dare say that I was happy. I had made peace somewhat with most of the demons from my past that had haunted me. The gospel and the Church had provided me with answers, healing, and hope. I had also grown to honor and respect my aunt and uncle. I was pained by the heartache I had inflicted upon them in my rebellious years. Although they did not support my going to America because they saw no safety net should I fail, they still respected my efforts. I was engaged in the pursuit of something I desired despite the opposition I had faced. They had grown to respect my opinion on matters of importance, especially religion, which was a subject of high popularity within the confines of the family. They nicknamed me "Pastor" for reasons I never asked about. I had surely come a long way from the quick steps of a volatile teenager to the lengthened stride of a stable young man, but the biggest accomplishment to my credit was my growth in love and concern for them, as I would have felt for my own parents. Even in the future, my aunt's helping hand would prove crucial to my success.

◧

Three months elapsed without a sign of a passport. I had contacted the embassy regularly with no favorable news. On one occasion I called the embassy and asked if my passport was there. The lady on the other end of the line asked my name, which I told her. She asked me to hold the line while she checked. After a minute she came back on the line and said, "It's here!" I was a bit surprised and doubtful, but I asked her if I could come and collect it, to which she responded affirmatively.

That afternoon I appeared at the embassy. A woman came out to the reception area to tell me that they did not offer services in the afternoon. I stated the reason for my presence, and she disappeared back into the office. She returned with a confused expression on her face. "I don't know who you talked to this morning, but there is no passport here in your name," she said. I was taken aback so thoroughly that the comic expression on my face must have qualified as a Kodak moment. To this day, I am still mystified at what was going on that day.

Two weeks later I heard from the Rwandan embassy again. They told me that the birth certificate I had provided was not valid. I reminded them that they had issued the birth certificate themselves. They told me that it must have been a mistake. They should not have done so in the first place because I had no proof that I was Rwandan. I would therefore not receive a passport. Their main question was how I, a Rwandan, could have a name like John Yves? Apparently it did not sound Rwandan.

I was devastated. I could not obtain a passport from Rwanda because I had no proof of citizenship, none from Zimbabwe since I had been under refugee status there, and definitely none from Belgium because our adoption and citizenship processes were still dragging on. I had finally been admitted to BYU and finally had the resources but was now hindered by what seemed a ridiculous turn of events. When I received this news, I was crushed.

Days later my aunt Godelieve asked me what the latest was with the passport. When I told her what had transpired she seemed lost in thought. Then she said, "You know, there may still be a way." She explained that three or four years earlier she had asked one of her sisters who still lived in Rwanda to obtain a document from my late father's prefecture. It certified that as children of my father, who was a citizen of that prefecture, my siblings and I had the same standing and were therefore Rwandans. This was a document that had been issued by the Rwandan authorities. My aunt had intended to use it for our adoption but had later learned that she did not need to. It had been sitting idle in her files for three or four years.

If that was not a miracle, then I fail to recognize what else it was. I took that document with me to the embassy, and three months later, about three weeks before my scheduled departure date, my passport arrived. Regina was so excited that she went to collect it on my behalf. It had been six long months during which I had been under constant pressure, imagining a scenario in which my departure would be delayed or worse. My aspirations had been under threat, usually on the brink of failure.

I applied for my visa at the American embassy, went for the interview, and obtained a five-year visa. Afterward it hit me that in a matter of days I was actually going to leave for America. It was not just a maybe anymore but a definite fact. The dream that I had nursed for the past decade was finally coming true. Words are inadequate to fully capture the intensity of the sensations that emanate from your core when the one thing your heart has pursued finally finds its way into your ambitious embrace. I had felt heavily crushed by all the sour disappointments I had tasted, all the humbling defeats I had suffered, and all the passionate tears I had shed. It had been a perilous journey, but I had endured, and now the success that had become a friend to me outshone all past failures.

My mind was already adjusting itself to my new lot, and I found myself looking retrospectively at my stay in Belgium, even before I left it. I held the country in high esteem, for it had become my home. My family lived there, and we were close to my aunt Annonciata and her children, our neighbors in the Netherlands. Every summer we had found our way to the Netherlands to relive the good old days in Zimbabwe with our cousins. I had a lot of history there. The worst temptations of adolescence had beset me here, the snares of the typical teenage identity crisis, which distorted my vision of what was important and what were exaggerated trifles. I had known deep sorrows but deep joys also. It seemed that my journey had forged qualities and refined traits in my character. It had demanded patience in the face of staggering bureaucratic inertia; it had required persistence when giving up was the most appealing option; it had required faith when the way was obscured by harsh reality. I walked away a patient and persistent and faithful man, an even bigger dreamer than I had heretofore been. It dawned on me finally that leaving for America was only a bonus. The real prize had been hidden in the adventure and experience. What a comforting lesson to learn from life, that no tragedy that had ever befallen me had failed to deliver a compensatory opportunity for growth and learning. My difficulty always lay in perceiving opportunity when grief abounded.

So many times I had forgotten the miracles that had made my life possible: our successful escape from Rwanda, the benevolent man from Zaire who carried Angel on his back and honestly exchanged our money, attending school in Zimbabwe and learning English, getting to Belgium to reunite with my family, the American man who paid for my SAT test with his credit card, my aunt remembering the document that proved our Rwandan citizenship—the list goes on.

Then there is the crowning blessing: running into two Latter-day Saint missionaries when I went to that basketball tournament. I believe that the rest of my life will have direction because of that particular encounter. The Latter-day Saint faith gave meaning to my life. I have mentioned that when I was a teenager many unanswered questions circulated in my mind regarding God and His role in my life. Fortunately, with time I received some answers, even though some were of my own speculation.

The Latter-day Saint faith teaches that our experience on

earth is but a small flash of our overall existence. We lived for eons of time before we came to this earth, and we will live forever after we have left the earth. Because of our premortal lives, we already have a formed personality, intelligence, attitudes, goals, and ambitions upon entrance into this world. This teaching rings true to me because though I have led close to the same life as my siblings, we are very different indeed and respond differently to similar circumstances. Each one of us is unique with different interests because we were who we were long before we came to this earth.

At some point in our lives, we must pause to ponder the meaning of our life in light of the experiences that have contributed to the formation of our character. For me, the question arose: Why do we have the experiences that we do? My attempt to answer this question has been formed from the following Christian standpoint:

I believe that we are on this earth for a purpose that will contribute, in some small way, to humanity, though that humanity may be as small as the circle of your friends or family. Many times in my life I have had impressions or feelings that drew me to do some benevolent act. I have even had opportunities to use my unique talents or abilities to help my fellowman. Sometimes I have heeded those calls and acted upon those impressions and felt God's approval through warm feelings in my heart. Other times I have ignored petitions for my help or my time for one reason or another and felt pangs of guilt as a result.

These and other experiences on earth are necessary for us to pass through in order to move from one level to the next. And so we are born to this earth, but at our birth, our past existence is veiled from our memory in order for us to learn from our earthly experiences. To that end, we have our lifetime to discover our personalities, attitudes, intelligence, and so forth in order to know who we truly are and to decide what we want to be.

How do we know who we truly are? Though we may believe otherwise, we do not really know ourselves until we see ourselves. But how do we see ourselves? There is an arrangement that allows us to see ourselves. The trials of our lives expose to us the strengths or weaknesses of our character. Trials are the mirror that allows us to see ourselves indeed, because trials, in whatever form, reveal to us how strong or weak we are. They are not always punishment for past offenses. Once we identify our weaknesses by virtue of those trials, we then have a choice to rectify them through the proper means. Trials are similar to a test. A test will not make us more intelligent, but it will reveal our standing in a subject, thus exposing which areas we need to improve.

In addition, through seeing our weaknesses, we also discover compassion for those with the same afflictions or who suffer through other afflictions. In essence, weaknesses are opportunities to strengthen character and build our ability to be more compassionate. I would probably not have known how independent I could be until I lost both my parents. As a teenager, I would not have known how weak my faith in the Divine was until I had been tried by all kinds of "bad luck." My Zambian mother, Regina, would not have known how strong she was until she had separated from her husband and was compelled to find a job and raise four children by herself. My aunt and uncle would not have known their incredible resilience until they had

John at the airport with Bishop Gardner and his wife, Marie-Jeanne.

lost everything they had spent a lifetime building and then were forced to start all over again with nothing in a foreign country. As I have heard it said, in the end our lives will fall into place; if they haven't, then it is not yet the end.

My last Sunday before my departure for America was a celebration indeed. Most of the people at church knew the difficulties I had faced, and a reception was held in my honor to bid me farewell. A book with photos of Belgium's finest monuments and landmarks was signed by every member of the congregation. The bishop presented the book to me before we proceeded to refreshments, and I spent the rest of the afternoon trying to talk to everyone who wanted to wish me the best. In fact, the cultural hall had been adorned with colored letters spelling, "Good luck, John!"

Before I left for home, Bishop Gardner sat me down to offer

advice. He told me that I was going to a very interesting state in America, one that exhibited relatively little cultural diversity. He told me to be mindful of that reality and to expect some adjusting. He reassured me that he would be at the airport to see me off, which he was.

My parting with my aunt and uncle was sad, and I noticed tears welling in my aunt's eyes that day at the airport. This was the first time I had seen her show emotion. I knew then that she cared for me very much, as my mother, her late younger sister, had cared for me. She wished me safety and luck. My uncle was as formal as always and wished me the best on my voyage. I thanked them for their hospitality and their support. My uncle gave me a copy of an aerial photo of the neighborhood that had been my home. On the back he had written, *"Voilà les photos de ton séjour en Belgique. Bonne chance en Amérique, ton troisième pays d'accueil,"* meaning, "Here are the pictures of your stay in Belgium. Good luck in America, your third country of residence." Saying good-bye to Angel and Mary was the music I did not want to face, the bitter cup from which I did not want to drink. I embraced them with much love and told them I was going to call them as often as I could. With those words I parted with my family.

Moments later, I relaxed in my airplane seat, fastened my seat belt, and leaned way back. I pushed out a long sigh and closed my eyes. I inhaled deeply to capture the essence of my presence in that moment. *I am here,* I thought to myself. *I am finally here.* And I exhaled.

I was caught in a trance of my own; I did not even notice the plane taxi out from the jetway, race down the runway, and lift into the air. But as it did, an overpowering sense of history

John's family farewell at the airport. From left to right: Uncle Felicien,
John, Bishop Gardner, Aunt Godelieve, Angel.

settled on me as I reflected and looked back on my life. I had been raised in situations where my qualifications for happiness had always been questioned and mostly discredited. Many a time, the mercilessness of life had humbled me to my knees. I had been evicted from the land of my inheritance by the barbarity of my fellowman; the sting of death had robbed me of my parents in my youth. Misery had been my companion from nearly the beginning of my existence. I had been told, "You can't do this; you can't do that. It's impossible!" I did not have the right story. I did not have the right background. Life had not dealt me the right cards. And so I leapt with my eyes shut tight and landed with my eyes wide open, enchanted by the beauty of hope. I had known a million reasons to concede defeat but only one to keep my grip on my dreams.

Hope had paved my way through the infernal snake pit with promise. Hope had kept my bare feet moving while I wandered in the desert of my travails. I had prevailed through hope, and I had found through my experiences both ordinary and miraculous the true Source of that hope. With hope I was now sailing into the oceans of opportunities; with those opportunities I could forsake pedestrian aspirations and soar into the heavens of greatness, a greatness of soul that whispers nothing but solace to the heart and for which all wrongs could be forgiven and all wounds healed. Then I could say that the past is gone, I have bled, and I have healed. All that was bruised is now only scars that I have to show for the life that I had led.

Never more will I say "Life is unfair!" For indeed it is—for everyone! Yes, for some more so than for others. But to those who cower in the face of affliction, it sadly remains so. Here I venture into this land of promise with a light in my eyes and fire in my heart, primed to fight bigger battles and bound to win more glorious victories. America, here I come!

As the plane flew toward the horizon, my joy abounded for what has been the life of a wayfaring man.